RANDY ELLISON

boys don't TELL

Ending the SILENCE
of Abuse

NEW YORK

boys don't TELL
Ending the SILENCE of Abuse

by Randy Ellison
© 2012 Randy Ellison. All rights reserved.

ISBN 978-1-61448-046-4 Paperback
ISBN 978-1-61448-047-1 eBook
Library of Congress Control Number 2011929414

Published by:
MORGAN JAMES PUBLISHING
The Entrepreneurial Publisher
5 Penn Plaza, 23rd Floor
New York City, New York 10001
(212) 655-5470 Office
(516) 908-4496 Fax
www.MorganJamesPublishing.com

Cover Design by:
Rachel Lopez
rachel@r2cdesign.com

Interior Design by:
Bonnie Bushman
bbushman@bresnan.net

Habitat for Humanity®
Peninsula Building Partner

In an effort to support local communities, raise awareness and funds, Morgan James Publishing donates one percent of all book sales for the life of each book to Habitat for Humanity. Get involved today, visit
www.HelpHabitatForHumanity.org.

To all the children in the world
who had their innocence ripped away from them.
May you find healing and be blessed with God's grace.

acknowledgements

First I would like to thank my therapist Dr. Karen McClintock. I don't think I would ever have made the recovery I have without your patient guidance and understanding. Thank you doesn't even come close.

Gracious thanks to my editor Judith Cope for making my scratchings first look like writing and then a book. You are great!

Thank you to my agent Michael Ebeling for saying yes and leading me into a whole new and strange world.

I need to mention friend Kelly Clark and his sidekick Tyler Vandemark. You guys are truly unsung heroes, yet you are such a big part of so many victims' recovery. Bless you both.

Next I want to thank my sisters, Candy Smith, Sharon Ellison and Monza Naff. Your loving support is more that anyone could ask.

And to my grandchildren Austin, Jack, Brady, Harper, Lily, and Daisy, thank you for giving me a good reason to seek recovery and health.

To my good friend Dee Anne Everson, thanks for dragging my victim self out into the world. It has changed my life experience more than you will ever know.

My daughters Katie and Maggie Ellison, what do I say? I'm sorry, I love you, and we have many good days ahead.

My wife and partner Helen, you are the best. Thanks for giving me so many chances in life and taking care of everything I was unable to cope with. I never could have made it without you.

contents

preface

We have a crisis, an epidemic of violence, secrets and lies. The estimated 20 million male victims and 30 million female victims are in every block, on every street in every town. Our society turns a blind eye, providing little help or solutions to those afflicted.

Our culture teaches us to be tough. We are told to "get over it, move on." That was what I tried to do after my first few months of therapy. But I found out victims of child sexual abuse can't just get over it. One never gets over it. And it takes a lot of work to move on. I hope this book will help them open their wounds so they may begin healing.

We are referred to as victim/survivors. Although I have always proudly thought of myself as a survivor, two years of counseling showed me that surviving is only the first step. I no longer want my identity to be that of a survivor. In order to be healed and whole again, I need to accept the part of me that was made a victim and incorporate him into who I am today.

It is also my hope that this book will help the public become aware of how the trauma of child sex abuse is ongoing, how the ramifications permeate and cripple the psyche until denial is at last cracked open and the healing process can begin. Creating such awareness may help change a culture that blames the victim as much or more than the perpetrator and hopefully precipitate a change in laws that let the criminals avoid prosecution. It is said that 90 percent of abuse cases are never reported. Of those reported cases, it is estimated that criminal charges are brought in 10-20 percent. That means we are prosecuting 1-2 percent of all offenses of child sexual abuse. While those numbers might be acceptable for purse snatching, they are shameful when it comes to protecting our children. Our society allows our children to be sexually abused while doing very little to stop it.

A swirl of media attention currently surrounds the handling of pedophiles in the Catholic Church, Mormon Church, Boy Scouts, schools, and elsewhere. As in my case, the institutions that employed these perpetrators turn to their lawyers to resolve these claims in an attempt to preserve their image. It is the resistance of these organizations that has forced a campaign of lawsuits in an attempt to get them to take responsibility and recognize their role in perpetuating a culture of abuse. If instead, these groups would apply their stated values when dealing with these cases, their image would fare better and they would be assisting the victims in healing.

After keeping secrets and telling lies to others and myself throughout my adulthood, I have found my voice. I have discovered that when I find the strength to speak my truth, it seems to give others permission to do the same and that helps us all heal.

Lastly, this book is written from my victim perspective. It represents my reactions to my process of recovery. It is not necessarily intended to be fair to the other people involved. Please understand and forgive that.

Chapter 1

the beginning of recovery

I didn't start this healing process until age 56. Prior to that, I had dissociated my abuser's behavior from the abuser. He was my friend, my mentor and my minister. I could not possibly think of him as a predator, so I detached the behavior from the person. This lasted for 40 years! My mother was the only person I might have ever trusted enough to tell, but she died when I was 21 and nowhere near ready to talk.

Even though, in my mind, I knew I had been abused, I spent three months in therapy before I could finally admit that my minister's behavior was criminal and I was in fact the victim. That was my first hurdle, and a very difficult one.

After those first few months in therapy, I said to my counselor "thank you very much, I'm okay now." She didn't attempt to dissuade me, but she did smile knowingly at me and suggested I might just leave the issues on the table for a while instead of trying to put them away again. She said it had been hidden away for so long it might be good to air it out a little more. She asked me to call her if I wanted to talk more. Two months later I was having troubled dreams. I called her and we resumed weekly appointments.

My next revelation was that what happened to me affected *every* part of my life: what kind of a husband I was, what kind of a father, what kind of a friend, and what kind of an employee. My abuse had triggered my withdrawal from society, my alcohol and drug addictions, my anger, my control issues, and, as a young adult, my thoughts of suicide. Any book on child sex abuse will list all of these traits and more as potential outcomes of abuse. As I continued sessions with my counselor, I was amazed to find how the tentacles of abuse and Post Traumatic Stress Disorder (PTSD) had permeated every aspect of my identity and my behavior. My superior attitude began to dissolve and I finally started growing again as a person.

Once the lights came on for me, every week was a new discovery of awareness. I have always enjoyed analyzing and am rarely surprised, so this was all new and even exciting to me. I began to look forward to the sessions and the understanding that came with each one. How emotionally moving and deeply satisfying it was to find that, buried under all the rubble and denial, I was in fact the person I thought I was but never showed to the world. I have had to learn to give myself permission to just be myself and to show my feelings, without fear of repercussion. I have found it most difficult to be open with those closest to me because I have hidden who I was and offered only an occasional glimpse of my true identity. Working to change patterns that have been embedded for so long has been extremely difficult, but the effort has rewarded me many times over. I see the difference in how people react to me and how I feel about my relationships. I have always been thought of as abrupt and a bit of an asshole. I have even taken pride in that. People I am around now find that image impossible to connect with me. Now I tend to be seen as a very caring person and I don't walk away with that bad feeling in my gut all the time, the way I used to.

After a few more months of therapy, and discovery of the depth of damage to my life I was able to write a letter (one I never intended to send) to my abuser to tell him how I felt. It was amazingly therapeutic to put my pain and hurt into words addressed to him. A couple of months after I wrote that letter, I decided to file a formal complaint with The Church and to include my letter to Pastor Jones. Since the Bishop was the most powerful person I could think of, I addressed the letter to him.

Dear Bishop,

I want to share something with you that I have never told a soul. I have barely admitted to myself it even happened. I grew up attending First Church. When I was in junior high school, Reverend Ronald Jones was hired as the Minister of Education at my church. He came with a reputation of being really good with kids. I looked forward to getting into the high school Youth Group to be able to take part, with him as leader. When I did join, I was pleased by the attention from and apparent friendship of Reverend Ron. I was insecure and having difficulty fitting in, and it felt wonderful to be so fully accepted.

A few short months later I was in his office complaining about my parents, school or maybe just life in general. Reverend Jones was consoling me and came over to rub my shoulders. It didn't seem inappropriate at that moment. Before I knew what was happening, he had his hands down my pants. The next thing I knew, my pants were down and he was performing oral sex on me.

I was 15 at the time and had no prior sexual experience. He was 40 and married with children. I pretty much had no idea what was going on. *My* minister, *his* office, *Christ's* church. I stayed involved in church and Youth Group in spite of this unexplainable turn in my Christian Education. Reverend Ron even got me a job as the evening and Saturday custodian. The reason is obvious at this point, but at the time I thought he was trying to help me.

Reverend Ron's private education lessons continued weekly for over three years. Through all those years I continued to think of him as my friend and mentor. Somehow my brain dissociated his sexual advances from the rest of our relationship. It is only after almost a year of therapy that I can admit he was a predator and be able to write this letter.

I have been married for 37 years and have two grown daughters and five grandchildren. I've had five different major careers in five different cities and have lived in 18 different homes. My life has been emotionally isolated and I have trusted no one. I have fought against anyone who tried to control me in any way. In fact, I developed strong control issues to make sure nobody ever got that much power over me ever again.

As a result of the advances of Reverend Jones, I have always questioned my sexuality. I wasn't attracted to men, so I knew I wasn't gay. In fact, my counselor has suggested I am probably homophobic. I have never related well to the "macho guy" image and behavior, so somewhere along the line I decided I was probably asexual. I'm guessing that all victims of abuse have extreme difficulty dealing with their sexuality due to the mixed messages they receive. Society says one thing about parental love and pastoral love, but sexual abuse crosses lines that leave the child totally confused, wondering where the lines really are.

I believe Reverend Jones should be confronted with my complaint together with a letter I am enclosing for you to read to him. No punishment would be too great for what he did. I believe there is a story in the Bible where Jesus says that anyone who hurts the children should have a stone put around his neck and be thrown into the sea.

Although I would not object to this, I think that at the very least the pastor's behavior should be made public and other victims sought out. People have a right to know when there is a predator like that is in their midst. Just as Christ did, you and The Church have a duty to put everyone on notice that there will be zero tolerance for anyone violating basic human values by abusing children.

Perhaps to show you this type of thing is not isolated, I also want to share with you an incident that took place at camp when I was 17. I was alone in the leadership cabin working on a program when Pastor Force came in and proceeded to chase me around the cabin trying to grab at me and kiss me. I was able to get away and run outside. I found Reverend Ron and told him what happened. He told me to just stay away from Pastor Force and let him know if it happened again. It never did, but once was enough. It scared me to death.

I hope you take this information as seriously as I do. The problem of sexual abuse of children has gone ignored and untreated for far too long, and unfortunately The Church is right in the middle of it. The impact of this abuse on both my family and me has been incalculable.

Sincerely,
Randy Ellison

Growing Up at First Church

Mama says I have to go to church
I ask her why; I've been going since I was a baby
I'm older now; haven't I learned enough
She says I need to learn to be more like Jesus
So I won't grow up like my papa
He's a drinker and he's crude, she says

I got no choice, so I go
Mostly geeks and freaks and me
Older kids form circles and sing and dance
The music draws them in
At the center I spy the Source
The Music Man, the Pied Piper
He writes the songs they sing
I wish I could join in
But I am too young and invisible

One day when I am old enough
He smiles that accepting smile at me and says welcome
I tell mama now I want to go to church
She says good
The Preacher Man will teach you well
He takes me by the hand and tells me I'm special
We talk of peace, love and acceptance
He listens to me
He makes my words into the music we sing
The Pied Piper is my friend

Mama says I'm on the right track
Now my life really means something
Things make sense
Mama's proud, I can tell

Then one day when I am low He rubs my shoulders
That's nice
Before I know what is happening

He touches places no one but me has touched
I don't understand
It doesn't seem right
But it feels good
As good as when I touch there at night alone in my room
My heart and mind say no
But I cannot find the words
Does that make me evil?

Over time it feels as though I am tied in that chair
And my mind travels far while He touches my skin
I can't say no to Him
And I sure can't tell mama
Music
    God
        Jesus
            Love
                Dance
                    Touch
                        Erection
                          Ejaculation

Do they really go together like that
I'm confused mama; what does it mean?

It was only after more than a year of counseling that I realized how my minister worked to make me feel important and adult-like, as though I were very special. I have since learned that this manipulation is called "grooming" and is almost always a part of sexual abuse of children. The abuser not only "grooms" the children, he grooms the adults and parents to make them all think how trustworthy and what a great guy he is. Sex offenders are generally master manipulators. It's all part of the abuse syndrome.

Below is the letter I wrote to Reverend Jones that I included with my letter to the Bishop. I never thought I would mail this letter or that anyone but me would ever read it. I asked that it be read aloud to Reverend Jones when he was confronted, so that it could be witnessed. I wanted someone to witness his reaction, and tell me about it, but I didn't want to be there.

Mr. Ronald Jones,

(I just can't bring myself to call you Pastor or Reverend.) This letter comes out of some writing I did recently after almost a year of therapy. I am currently dealing with emotional blocks resulting from my youth, attempting to come to terms with lifelong repercussions from the perversion and sexual abuse you perpetuated on me. I believe I owe it to myself to write this, and you owe it to me to read it.

What happens when an intelligent, sensitive 15-year-old boy is turned off and unchallenged at home and at school? In 1965 this boy turned to his talented minister. I was seduced by your energy and the respect you seemed to show me, the very qualities I was looking for in my parents and my teachers. I yearned to connect with an adult on a soulful level, exchanging ideas as equals. In my mind I was no longer a child. Unfortunately the relationship with you came to include your sexual pathology. Maybe for you it started there, but I would like to think not. As I write this though, I can't imagine how you could not have known long before you did anything to me; I believe that you knew you were headed there. Ron, I believe that you know how much you meant to me, and I can't get my mind, even 40 years later, to picture you as a predator. But if you knew ahead of time, then you were in fact a predator. Because of the power differential between us, and because of your position of spiritual authority, you are seriously accountable for that abuse.

Through all these years, I have been hanging on to all the benefits from the relationship we shared, and denied or disassociated the criminal behavior of which you are guilty. Until now, I simply never thought of it that way. I left it as an unsolvable paradox. Now that I am 56, I am left with the horrific truth that the person I loved, admired, felt closest to during my tough adolescent years was, in fact, a criminal predator…and I was one of his victims. You used your talent and charisma to seduce a vulnerable, disenfranchised adolescent to satisfy a perversion. I guess I can imagine an adult being attracted to a teenager, but I can't imagine acting on it. You obviously weren't as gifted as I thought you were! And certainly not as spiritually evolved, or you would never had misused your power the way you did. Ron, I didn't deserve to be so mis-used and abused by you.

When I was having trouble with my parents and didn't feel I could talk to them, what did you do? Work with the family? Encourage me to work things out? Did you show support for my parents or did you use my dissatisfaction to strengthen your relationship with me? I think the latter, definitely the latter. As I see it now, predators see that disconnect and step in to befriend and eventually abuse a vulnerable adolescent when he is struggling with acceptance and working on becoming an adult, when he is stuck back and forth between childhood and maturity like a 12-year-old boy's cracking voice.

Now I have to consider that you were seeing those things in me, coming up and putting your arm around me with the appearance of caring, but in reality you planned to include me in your perversion. No matter how innocently the process began, that was the result. Regardless of what else you offered, you cannot overcome the breach of trust you committed. As a talented leader of a spiritual community, whose job it is to be a faith leader and mentor to young people—using your gifts to gain the trust of a genuine love is way over the edge. It makes so little sense that I can only assume the perversion is the ultimate motivator from the beginning and all other behavior is used to feed it. Therefore: Predator. Whatever else, you are that. Can you tell how much trouble I'm having accepting this?

Now that I have accepted that fact and opened the door that was locked, my memories take on new meaning. For example, I remember you telling me that I was "that way." When the two gay men who owned the restaurant had been over to see you, you told me they could tell that I was like them. You said they could see it and feel it. You taught me homosexual signals, like wearing a pinky ring to show you were gay. You told me which ministers were gay. Were you actually schooling me to be gay? Were you recruiting? That time Pastor Force chased me around the cabin at camp and scared me to death, you told me just to stay away from him. Did you know about his desire to pursue me in advance, or did he just know about your involvement with me and assume he could have a little fun too?

Having to reconsider my entire history with you causes me enormous pain. It makes me profoundly sad. You went from the heights of respect and admiration to the depths of one of the most reviled crimes on earth—using a child for your sexual pleasure. Dear God, what switch did you turn off in your head to be able to do this? I really cannot imagine it! Do you know that I have never looked up to anyone since you and have never had an idol? Kind of put the old kibosh on dreams and aspirations.

Do you think the experience helped me become a better person or devoted Christian? Did it teach me trust, to love openly? Did it teach me to accept affection at face value? Was it representative of the values you preached about? Or was it total hypocrisy? Did it in fact teach me wall building? Does my lesson from you actually teach me that if someone is too nice, or acts in a caring way towards a child or a person in need, then they probably have ulterior motives and shouldn't be trusted?

Ron, the impact of your relationship with me is devastating. Unfortunately, it invalidates all the values you supposedly were charged to teach. How we victims deal with this forked-tongue message is to mistrust all expressions of affection, love, or verbalized appreciation. I became a cynic and wary of all people who want to get too close. I've got walls behind walls. Now that I think of it, I don't believe I have ever let anyone inside since you were inside my mind and soul and distorted everything. Have you ever thought of it that way?

Somehow, with the aid of a selective memory and the gifts of my own character, I am grateful that I got the lessons and true values of Christian love (probably because of my family) and merely came away cynical from the lies and deceit within your abuses of genuine affection.

But the devastating results of having never processed the lies are still with me. Until now, I merely grouped together all perversions of what might actually be of worth and filed them away under "Adults Abuse Values." This includes messages I got from Mom and Dad: "Always do your best...you can always improve... nothing you do will ever be enough...accomplish something every day...never be ashamed of mistakes, the only mistake to be ashamed of is the one you don't learn from." Although some of those messages have worth, when I look at the overwhelming pressure in them I say, "Gosh, wonder why I'm so over-the-top driven? No wonder I am now asking, when does the fun start? I guess at 5 o'clock when the alcohol and/or drugs get rolling."

What did I miss? What did you take away from me besides my innocence? What did I not experience because of your dominance and influence in my life? What have I missed over the years because I couldn't open myself up for the experience? You stole my trust. I guess that's one reason society is so emotional about this crime. I am a strong survivor, but I can't begin to calculate where my life might have gone if I weren't restricted by the walls I built to protect myself from people like you. What if I had been weaker and it had destroyed me? How could you know that wouldn't happen? Did you care? Have you ever, in all these years, even once considered the consequences of your choices on *my* life?

I want to make this clear: You are not the cause of all my life's problems, by any means. But you certainly threw some major hurdles my way that I did nothing to deserve. The hurt you caused me has lasted a lifetime.

I wonder how many other boys you abused. I wonder, if they were not as strong as I am, if their lives were destroyed by it, like so many I have read about? I don't know what reaction you will have to all I am saying to you. To be honest, I don't care anymore. I gave up on that when I never heard from you. All the years I waited, carrying this secret around. If you were the person you pretended to be, the person I thought you were, I would have heard from you by now. My counselor says that I am naïve to think that you would take responsibility, reach out to make amends to me. Probably so, but I guess I should be happy I have a little of that innocence left. Right now I am primarily concerned that this process of truth telling serves me and my health. I can now truly leave your process in God's hands.

I intend to spend the rest of my life learning to take down walls, learning to trust again, and to believe once more in the possibility of truly reciprocal love. I know I can't get back what you took away, but I can work to make things better for others, to help my grandchildren grow up unafraid of being used by adults in their lives.

A former friend you used and abused for personal indulgence and satisfaction,

Randy

bastard

PEACE   working for and living
LOVING   our brothers and sisters
EQUALITY   of all people
SHARING   your bounty with others
HELPING   friends and strangers alike
FAITH   in the existence of a greater power
BELIEVE   in the inherent goodness of all God's creations
DIGNITY   act with and *always* treat others with
HOPE   that one day all the earth will know peace

These were not just words and phases
They were the air I breathed
They pulsed through my veins
My beliefs and values
They filled my head and heart
They weren't just my foundation
They were who I was
You recognized me
You saw all that goodness
And you wanted it
So young, so fresh, so pure

You wanted to possess it
You wanted to control it
Your pain, your perversion and your greed took over
You crushed my innocence with the heal of your boot
Just as you would have a cigarette butt
You used and abused my trust to the point of depletion
You replaced my optimism with sarcasm and skepticism
I became an alcoholic and a drug addict
I hid from people every way I could
Even my own family
You forced me to lock it all away
The good and the bad...ME
Today I mourn the enormity of that loss
You bastard!

I find it interesting that the above perspective comes forty years later and after a year of therapy. In the early years, after the abuse had ended, I still thought of Reverend Ron as my friend. I would visit him occasionally when I was home from college. He took part in my wedding and he even spoke at my mother's funeral. There was such a complete compartmentalization and dissociation separating the abuse from our relationship that I never put it together. Somehow I, and others like me, *lock the horrors away so we can go about our daily lives without completely falling apart.* It's one thing to deal with abuse by a stranger, it is quite another to deal with abuse by a loved one that we either live with or see regularly.

[*Almost two years have passed since I wrote to Reverend Ron. I am a different person now. I do not feel like a victim anymore. I have fewer addictions, and the ones that are left have less of a grip on me. I spend more time with my wife Helen and my grandkids. I feel better mentally and physically and have more confidence. Three years of therapy have helped to transform my life. So it's finally time to write it all out.*]

Bein' Cool, Not So Much

Today I officially started my book
Felt accomplished for two days
Tellin' the victim's story
Bein' the hammer of God

Went to church today
I don't know if the preacher is psychic
Or if her biorhythms are in tune with mine
Or if some higher power
Is linin' things up or what

But I have to sit and listen to a sermon
'bout Peter wantin' Jesus to be cool
Take His rightful place
Like a king

But ol' Jesus says no way
He's gotta suffer

Actin' cool just ain't cool
Humble's the way

The preacher says we try too hard to be individuals
Misses the point
We are one
All part of the whole

After I finished writin' chapter one
I felt like a king
My ego out front
Leadin' the way
Tellin' *my* story
How Cool am I?

Damn preacher gotta get in the way
Remind me
It ain't just my story

Damn, I forgot
It's about millions suffering
It's tellin' their story too
Balancing the scales
Showing what the evil does to kids
How it stays with you
Eats up part of your insides

Gotta remember to say thanks to the preacher
And keep goin' back
Help keep me on track
Amen

Chapter 2

revelation

I was 48 years old with a well-paying job as a lumber broker, but it wasn't satisfying and I figured there had to be a better way to live. Whenever I ate a meal, I would get an upset stomach and have to go to the bathroom within minutes. This pattern had been going on to a lesser degree since I was young, but now it was becoming a serious problem.

I went to a doctor who had me take a barium test, where you have to drink a liquid and watch on an x-ray machine as it goes through your system. The test indicates how long your body takes to process food. They told me to expect the test to take one to two hours, but the chemical went through my system in 17 minutes. As a result, the lab techs nicknamed me "rapid transit." The doctor's response was to prescribe Zoloft to numb my emotions and dissatisfaction with my job and life. With some indignation I said no thank you.

Not long after I turned down the Zoloft, the vice president at my company told me the president and chairman had wondered why I was being paid management money above my commissions. They insinuated I had cheated in order to be paid more, when in fact the president himself had approved the bonus override one year earlier for all the extra work I had performed. He must have forgotten that when he was going over the profits and losses for the year, which weren't up to par.

That night I went home and told Helen I was going to quit. It was the Ides of March. I became totally depressed and started getting stoned before work and at lunch every day. Nobody seemed to notice. Certainly no one ever said anything to me about looking or acting different. Surprisingly, my sales income stayed about the same. I continue getting loaded until I quit one year later to the day on the Ides of March. I guess that as a survivor, I had adapted to an altered reality without anyone, including myself, even noticing. In hindsight it is pretty interesting that after being totally offended by the doctor's offer of mood altering medication I turned around and used one of my own. We moved away—again. At age 49 I began rebuilding old houses for a living. No more bosses. No more working with others. Do it all. Do it alone.

Eight years later I had learned plumbing, wiring, roofing, carpentry, and painting. Together with my wife I completely rebuilt and sold three houses. I was still unfulfilled. Something was missing, but I didn't know what.

Late one night, in the middle of winter, I got a call from my daughter. She said my grandson, who had been having problems since his parents separated, was throwing a tantrum. He had awakened his younger brother and sister. My daughter took the younger kids into her room and locked the door. Out of total frustration she told her son the police were coming.

When I got to my daughter's house I found my nine year old grandson hiding in his closet, standing there in his underwear, face as white as a sheet. I suppose he imagined the cops had arrived to haul him away. The fear in his face and his vulnerability broke the wall inside me. What I saw in his rigid body and face was the same terror of the unknown I had felt those many years ago when I was totally powerless and scared to death with no hope of protecting myself or stopping what my abuser was doing. It all came rushing back to life; the long-suppressed feeling of being overpowered both physically and emotionally by someone I had totally trusted and actually revered.

I lifted my grandson up into my arms, sat down on his bed, and cradled and rocked him. I told him everything would be okay. I told him I would always make sure he was safe and I would never let anybody hurt him. I'm positive I was saying those words to the young boy inside me as much as my grandson. I told him anytime he was scared all he had to do was call and I would be there for him. I would do everything in my power to see that no one did anything to him to make him feel as powerless and afraid as I had felt as an adolescent.

My defensive wall had cracked; my denial was replaced with an inkling of awareness. A few weeks later I went to see a minister I knew. I talked to him about being molested as a teenager and he referred me to a counselor who specializes in abuse. The first nine months of counseling got me to the point of filing my complaint with The Church.

As difficult as those months were, I entered a whole new territory when it came time to tell my truth to The Church in person. They had requested that I come to the district office, but I declined and asked that I be allowed to tell my story in the relative security of my home. As fate would have it, it was Epiphany Sunday, January 2007. Two district superintendents, regional supervisors who reported directly to the Bishop, came to my home. One was second in command to the Bishop in the state. The other flew in to witness and take notes. Surrounded by the love and presence of my wife and two of my sisters, I told what had happened to me and answered their questions with relative calm. I even weathered the three cell phone calls one Inquisitor took from her teenage daughter who had accompanied her and was shopping downtown. Evidently she felt these calls were important enough to interrupt my account of the trauma I had buried in my unconscious mind for so long. After a couple of hours, we took a break for coffee. My wife overheard Mr. Inquisitor say under his breath, "May god have mercy on our souls."

Upon returning, I told them I wanted to play some songs from a record album Reverend Jones made when I was a teenager. Mrs. Inquisitor tried to object, but I insisted. Several of the songs were based on words I had spoken to my minister; he had put them to music and had woven verses of affection for me into them. The album included two poems he had written to me, poems I only understand now after a year of therapy. At the time he gave them to me, I think they scared me and I just took them home and put them away. One of the songs was "dedicated to Randy who came to me with friendship unlimited."

After playing the songs and giving my visitors copies of the words, I showed them the album cover. Mrs. Inquisitor was pretty disgusted by then. When she saw the faded inscription on the plain white cover—"Randy, There are no more words…Ronald"—she practically threw the cover to Mr. Inquisitor in disgust.

I had turned things over to The Church looking for justice. After the Inquisitors left, I went upstairs and took the longest hot shower of my life. I don't know if I was feeling dirty or what, but I needed to wash whatever it was off me.

You know how they talk about postpartum depression? Welcome to post-trauma depression, which was probably PTSD. I have never functioned at a lower level than during those four weeks following my meeting with the

Inquisitors on Epiphany Sunday. I cried a lot, sometimes for an hour or more at a time. It's as though the years of locked-up emotion came pouring out. Once I opened the dam, I couldn't stop it.

After having this huge awakening and experience of truth-telling, I wanted to share with other family members, so I traveled to Wisconsin to tell my daughter and to Oakland to tell my niece. Yet nothing seemed to have changed. The church wanted Reverend Ron to get some counseling and be healed. They will talk to about 20 or 30 people to see if there is anything else to cover. Oh, and by the way, they want him to reimburse me for my counseling. Gee, thanks.

It was on my way to Wisconsin that I wrote my first "poem." I call it "poetry" because I found a definition online that seemed appropriate. Wordsworth said that "poetry is the spontaneous overflow of powerful feelings" and I was certainly having powerful feelings and they were overflowing. I was trying to find a way to express what was going on inside of me to my daughter, a person who had known me all her life, yet not known me at all.

Secrets and Lies

What happens when we distort the truth
    and store it as lies in our mind?
To protect the Lie we construct smaller lies
    and place them around it like a bunker
We try not to go there, fearing something will change
    and the monsters will get out
In our zeal for safety we keep others far away,
    hoping they won't notice our fortress
As the years pass we check on things…
    they look the same… All Clear

Change is so gradual, we take no notice
    of the increased weight of our burden
Life goes on. We are not aware of the pieces
    now behind the walls
Given enough time, our secret and its guardians
    work their way to our center

As the inner fortress expands we lose more
      of ourselves to its growing hunger
Where our heart once beat is now a war zone
      dominated by our defenses

We hold up a cardboard cut-out so the world
      doesn't notice our missing pieces and lies
We can't understand when friends and family
      don't recognize us or tell us we've changed
Until one day we look in a mirror
      and we don't recognize ourselves

The initial elation I felt after talking to the Inquisitors and being freed of my secret was short lived. I couldn't work for two months. I caught every bug that came along. I couldn't focus on anything. Leaving town only helped a little and then it was back to nothing. Even getting high wasn't satisfying. I just waited. Waited for what? Something to make me feel better; something to represent the ordeal I had been through. Couldn't they put him in a stockade in the public square for all to see? It seemed like people ought to be talking about this instead of what Brittany Spears or Paris Hilton did yesterday.

Unnamed

What do you call something
That is so horrific
That you totally block it
A part of your brain knows it happened
It's just that it's not supposed to happen
So your brain says it didn't happen
You create a space for it
No label
Just like an unmarked grave
Because if it had a name
Then it would have meaning
And everything else in the world

Would have to be a lie
Dissociation they call it

Daddy loves me
My preacher works for God
They wouldn't do anything to hurt me
My teacher is trying to help me
Respect your elders
Adults know best

I know they love me
So they wouldn't do anything
That was bad for me.
The unnamed has to stay hidden
Or nothing else makes sense

Helen and I leave town about every seven days. On one trip to the beach, she told me she needed to talk about her anger. In response, on our first night away, I proceeded to get thoroughly smashed and passed out by nine. The next day we talked. She shared her resentment about my withholding information from her about my abuse. Believing the withholding has had a major impact on our life, she now wondered what else I "have not told her." I explained that I was not aware of hiding anything. When I told her early in our relationship about Ron molesting me, I thought of it as disclosure. Helen thought it was something that happened once or twice. I tried to explain how, in those days, I was still protecting my abuser and, unable to tell her more and just could not discuss it any further. The thought that Ron could be a child molester and not the wonderful religious leader I (and everyone else) thought he was, was more than I could handle.

Our discussion led to talking about our lack of intimacy. Helen seems to relate to intimacy as honest sharing. I see intimacy as touching, snuggling and nurturing. I believe that is part of why I was drawn to her. She did not threaten my walls. Call it karma or blind luck, but she is the best thing that ever happened to me. We are total opposites, which means we daily have the benefit of learning about life from another perspective, or just be pissed off. We argue, we fight, we compromise and sometimes if we are lucky we learn.

One Sunday Helen went to church with me. When a youth choir sang a song about peace and love, I cried. I remembered those feelings as an idealistic youth, but in church that day I realized I couldn't feel the joy in them anymore. It made me feel cold and sick. The experience with Reverend Ron cut me off from that joy and idealism, and triggered my becoming an invisible person. I had hidden my faith and soul from everyone for all of my adult life. He robbed me of the joy I had once felt over so many things.

Fear and Confusion

I built my walls high
Filled them with concrete and rebar
Thinking it made me strong
I could have just pulled the blinds
The result would have been the same
The extra protection only eased my mind
Hiding is hiding

I dream of being attacked and cry out "h e l p!"
I can't get away
Helen wakes me
Sometimes I get up to walk it off

Sometimes in the dream
I can fly to get away
To a place I am not threatened

I am always watching
I notice how people touch
Is it playful
Is it caring
Is it loving
Is it suggestive
Is it nasty
Is it controlling
Touch is scary...
It's also a longing

I freak out if I think someone is trying to control me
Or get too close
What do they want
What is their motive
Trust has a *very* short leash

Maintain full independence
Don't rely on others
Disappointment at best
Betrayal at worst
Cynical? You bet!

I have lived with fear every day
Only I didn't recognize it
I thought the banner on my fortress said *Fearless*
But in reality it said *Scared*

Chapter 3

learning to live with it

This week I get a massage from my therapist daughter Katie, who comments that she thinks no one could go through something like I am going through and not get bodywork. My body has been extremely tense. I don't know how much tension is from the emotions and how much is from drug withdrawal. I am sure the leg twitches are due to emotional release. For about six weeks now my legs have been involuntarily twitching when I go to sleep and during the night. I mean major tremors. It seems as though it is a physical release of all that I have been holding. During my truth-telling, my sisters had talked of releasing the toxins through my lower chakras back into the earth. It makes sense that I would hold my emotions there. That's how I would like to think of it anyway.

Next I go to the chiropractor. My left knee is out, my neck is out, and everything in between. The Chiropractor asks what I have been doing to mess up my body to that degree. I tell him it is just my body wanting to be healed. Then I go to the doctor for a physical for the first time in over two years. I think I have prostate cancer, that my carotid arteries are blocked, and that any day now I will have a stroke. I was imagining which would be worse, chemotherapy or being paralyzed and having to rely on others to do everything for me!

But after the physical, the doctor tells me my heart and lungs sound fine. I have excellent circulation to my feet and my neck arteries are clear. My prostate is quite fine except perhaps a little enlarged, for which he prescribes ten days of antibiotics. No cancer, no stroke, no invalid. Two days later he calls with the lab results. The tests show a little inflammation for which he suggests fish oil. He says my sugar count is high (pre-diabetes) and I will have to cut out sweets and watch my weight. Then he delivers the killer blow—my liver function is low. My SGOT is 47 (normal 10-42) and my SGPT is 114 (normal 5-40). I have never heard of SGPT or SGOT, so I'm not that impressed.

But when he starts saying things like "alcoholic hepatitis," scarring of the liver that never functions again, and eventual cirrhosis of the liver, he has my attention. He wants me to stop drinking for two to four weeks and then take the test again. Now I normally start drinking around 5:30 or 6, that is if I don't have a Bloody Mary with breakfast. I usually have two or three glasses of wine every evening, sometimes preceded by a double bourbon and water. I think it's fair to call three ounces of liquor a double. A generous double, but a double nonetheless. Anyway, I don't know of anything called a "triple" except in baseball. Generally I spread the drinking over enough time that I don't get "drunk" but I sure get a good buzz. Since I quit smoking pot a couple of months ago, the alcohol is not nearly as satisfying though.

Helen says she will quit with me. She has been talking about quitting anyway to help with her weight loss. Since she had just offered me a drink before the doctor called, she suggests that we quit tomorrow. GREAT idea!

Then I call my smoking and drinking partner brother-in-law and tell him the news. Since this is a regular topic for us he is very supportive. We decide that the six or so ibuprofen I take each day is probably contributing to the liver problems. Okay, now we're on to something. Perhaps the alcohol is not the sole culprit. At one point we actually decide I should try cutting out the ibuprofen for a month, keep drinking (in moderation of course!) and then see what the test would show. In the end, he suggests that maybe it wouldn't be such a bad thing to quit drinking daily (easy for him to say). Drinking may seem enjoyable, but it isn't really worth dying for. Philosophically I have to agree with him. Nobody told me that facing the trauma I experienced as an adolescent would end up leaving me clean and straight!

I wake up this morning thinking I will go online and really research SGPT and SGOT and also the ibuprofen thing. In the end I don't do it. Somehow reason settles in and the message is clear. You drink way too much and have been rationalizing it for far too long. So no Bloody Mary with breakfast and no wine tonight. One day at a time. The Serenity Prayer comes to mind.

God, grant me the serenity to accept the things I cannot change;
Courage to change the things I can;
And wisdom to know the difference.

Inner Strength

I went to therapy to reveal my secrets
Coming to terms with them as it were
It was harder than I imagined
I thought it would make me stronger
(Drain the cyst don't ya know)
It left me feeling empty
I had held secrets so long
It was like cutting a part of me out
Poison as it was.

The next step
Was to deal with my addictions
I knew I had to
Not only for myself
But so I could reconnect
With my loved ones
And the real world

This step is almost harder
I love my addictions
They have been my best friends
For a long, long time
They comfort me
As no human can
They give me strength to go on
When I can find none in my own body
When I am down
They are always there to pick me up
They help me connect to my world,
And to my God
Absent of other humans
My solutions
Are as close as the cupboard
Or the drawer
Just plug in

So quick
So easy
So satisfying

Now that I'm close [to being free]
An interesting thing has happened
The stronger side of my body
My left side
Has lost its strength
It started in my knee
Then my hamstring
Doc gave me pain medication for that
Nice
Told me it would take six weeks to heal
Take my pills and rest
(I did have the sense to turn the pills over to my wife)
Four days later I broke a tooth on the upper left
Connected?
Maybe not
But strange I think
I kinda like the woo-woo stuff
This seems a bit of a stretch
And yet it doesn't
If I remove my artificial power
That I have relied on
All my life
It makes sense
That I might fall down

As much as I know the many reasons to quit
Not only quality of life
But life itself
There seems to be a small part of me
That whispers "nooooo"
So on it stretches
Off for a week to a month or two
Then a little slip

For a day or a week
Been goin like that for over nine months now
Gettin' old
Do it or don't
But back and forth is just another lie
It gets harder each time
And as I remember
I started all this to get rid of the lies

So I start goin' to A.A.
Hard at first
They weren't like me
They hadn't lived through what I had
On my first visit
They did give me
A 24-hour sober coin
They passed it around the room
And everyone pressed energy into it
Between their palms
I must say it did give me strength

Been goin' three weeks now
And I'm surprised
At how much smarter they're gettin'
And surprisingly
I'm finding a lot of similarities
Between them and me
Survival means slow death
Letting go means life

I think it's time
To kill off the me
That relies on chemical stimulants
And perceived inner strength
Move out of the survival mode
Admit that I am not an island unto myself
Learn to use the strength

> I gain from relationships with others
> And from God
> Learn to walk and talk again
> And find a life worth living

This theme of working on my addictions repeats itself over and over in my story because that's the way life is. Just because I have a self-awakening it does not mean all my problems are solved, far from it. It just means they are out in the open so I can work on them. And work on them I do.

As time has gone on it has occurred to me that the most important part of life is to show up, both physically and mentally. I find if I am truly present, it is amazing what can happen

I Want to Be Present

> I'm tired of hiding
> I checked out—absent
> Ruled by fear and addictions
> That's why we use, isn't it?
> To go somewhere else
> Anywhere but here
>
> It is to my great shame
> That I admit
> I was not present for my children
> I am so sorry girls
>
> I am surrounded by things I love
> I want to experience them
> When loved ones are here
> I want to be with them
> I don't want to check out anymore
> I want to be involved with my grandkids
> There are lots of things I want to do
> I need to be present
> I want to be present

Chapter 4

reality sucks

We just got back from vacation in San Diego with the entire family, plus my sister-in-law and nephew. It was great to have 12 of us together for six days and nights. One child and one adult had different types of the flu. Yeah, baby! I drank every night. And right in the middle of the vacation, I received an email saying Reverend Ron might lose his license. I didn't tell anybody, I just got drunk, whopping drunk! I woke up at 12:30 am with the worst migraine headache I have ever had. I felt as though I was going to explode. Overload. Overload. Lookout captain, I think she's going to blow!

Earlier today I returned a call from Mrs. Inquisitor. She says that the Bishop met with Ron last week and told him that if the abuse had been reported at the time it was occurring, it would have been a felony. He said Ron could either turn in his license or face a Church court trial. He agreed to turn in his license. After the Regional Conference receives the license, the Bishop will send a letter to all church members of the Conference, pastors and lay people, to inform them that Ron had "Withdrawn under Complaint" for sexual misconduct. Boy, that almost covers it, doesn't it? I asked Mrs. Inquisitor if that was it? She said she wanted to see me reimbursed for counseling expenses, but yes, that's it. I told her I had been paying for this for 40 years and I wasn't ready to accept this as the final outcome.

Before I found myself in this position I had always felt that people should put problems of youth, including abuse, behind them. Big deal. Get over it. Move on. Right? Wrong! Until we can open that box and shed light on the abuse, we *don't have a clue as to its impact*. We don't know how to begin to change our lives to become the person we are truly meant to be, the person we are inside, the person we know we are, and can't figure out why others don't. I have always been totally offended when others mistakenly assumed who I was. How could they possibly assume I would think this, or do that? This "insult" seems pretty absurd after I realized I have been hiding who I am for most of my life. As a young adolescent I naturally tried to hide my true feelings so I could be cool and be accepted by my peers. Then I found church and youth group, a place to be accepted for myself. Once I became a victim, the lesson was clear. There is *no safe place. Always be on guard and protect yourself.* That became my motto for life.

I just read a quote on the Internet that helps me understand a little of my process in repressing all of this. "You can make sense of sexual abuse and no God, or God and no sexual abuse. But how do you tolerate the two realities together?" [1]

I have always had a strong belief in God, a strong faith. How could my minister, God's anointed One, sexually abuse me? In my mind, he couldn't. When our minds come across an unsolvable paradox, we use any means, illogical or otherwise, to accept the more palatable part and dismiss the less believable. I retained memories of these acts, I just never saw them as sexual abuse. Although on some level I knew it was wrong, somehow I was able to disassociate the abuse from the perpetrator. If anything, I felt shame myself. In processing all of this, I think I actually have been waiting for my spiritual mentor to explain how this all happened and fix it somehow.

I am still amazed and even a little chagrinned by how simple and childish these thoughts are, but I have to keep in mind that I interpreted and stored all these memories with the tools of a naive adolescent. For that very reason, the impact of these events cannot be underestimated.

I continue to be surprised at the complexity and ramifications of the abuse. Now a grandfather, I am reviewing the memories I had as a 16 year-old, memories I accepted and believed until recently. Now I find them to be so distorted as to have turned my life 90 degrees off. What I thought was north, I now find is really east, and so on.

As I look back, I wonder how I could ever know how much of my life has been impacted by the abuse. I recently remembered the thoughts of suicide I

---

1 Diane Langberg, "On the Threshold of Hope"

had as a young person, thoughts that lasted into my late twenties. Overcome with despair, I felt I was going crazy, with no concept or understanding of what life was all about. I even planned how I would do it. My minister destroyed my faith and the foundation of my belief system.

At that point my final response was to "toughen up" and just do it (life). I taught myself to control the negative and "crazy "thoughts. Eventually my mind stopped going there. As I look back I can picture myself, with the ball in my hands, running down the field rarely letting anyone close enough to touch me, let alone tackle me.

What is the punishment for stealing the peace and grace of God from a child?

This morning my wife wondered aloud if we will make it together. I knew that by choosing to confront my inner demons I might be putting my entire life as well as our marriage at risk. But it scares the hell out of me to hear her say it out loud.

Chapter 5

the official response

Today I received a copy of a letter the Bishop sent to all the clergy in the Regional Conference. It is the culmination of the complaint I made regarding the sexual abuse I suffered over a three-year period in the 1960s. I am disappointed and saddened by this bland corporate response to a crime against God and children. Across the center of the letter was stamped:

CONFIDENTIAL

Below are quoted excerpts from the Bishop's letter and my responses to them. I have highlighted in boldface the phrases that most wounded and angered me.

I am deeply saddened as I write this letter…This letter is to be **regarded as confidential.** I would appreciate it if you would **not copy this letter** for transmission to a wider audience…

The message here is clear: let's keep this quiet. No, we are not going to go to individual churches and talk about this, nor are we going to look for other victims. Tell a few people in whispers if you must, but please do not duplicate this for distribution.

Reverend Jones **confessed** to the allocation of **sexual misconduct,** acknowledging that by his actions he **violated** the **sacred trust** of the ministerial office.

Okay, here is a self-admitted pedophile who committed felonies in his church office. A man who in his forties sexually and mentally abused a teenage boy who was under his care as Youth Pastor and Religious Leader of a mainline church. I think using the phrase "allocation of sexual misconduct" is just a tad light and does not give the slightest indication of the man's actual crimes. Where is the outrage? Where is the Bishop's admonition to the church community that a faith leader has used his position to abuse a child of Christ?

> In February, Rev. Jones voluntarily **surrendered the credentials** of his ministerial office **under complaints**…He now **assumes a different role** as a lay member of a local church, which **he selected** in consultation with the pastor of that church…

Are you kidding me? *He selected* a different role in consultation with his pastor? Was the church told he is a pedophile? Does he have restrictions placed on him as to his association with children? Are you acting to protect the community, or is your underlying motivation one of self-protection?

We are affected in profound ways.

Let me tell you about "being affected in profound ways." I have moved my wife and two daughters 18 times to five different cities and have had five different careers. My life and my relationship with my wife have suffered immeasurably. Both of my daughters are living with the results of my distortions and both are affected in profound ways. I can't begin to imagine how my shame has worked its way into their lives and the lives of my five grandchildren, but I know it has. I have just read about a new research finding that Post Traumatic Stress Disorder can leave emotional scares that can change our DNA and are passed on genetically to our children.[2] How's that for profound?

> Please hold the **victim** of this incident of clergy sexual misconduct as well as **Ronald Jones** and **his family** in your prayers.

---

2 Isabelle Mansuy, of the University of Zurich, published in *Biological Psychiatry*, 2010.

We pray for the perpetrator and *his* family, but not for the family of his victim. Trust me, if you lived through the abuse I did, you would not call it an "incident of sexual misconduct" and your prayers would be that this never happen to anyone in your family.

After so many years of hiding, shame and denial, and a year of counseling, I decided to make a formal complaint to The Church where I was abused. I told my darkest secrets to my family and to strangers (Mr. And Mrs. Inquisitor). I have cried rivers and had many sleepless nights. My hope had been that The Church would "do the right thing." Instead, I believe they took the most minimal route they could find. They came and put their big toe in the lake of my despair instead of jumping in with me. They responded as a corporation, not as representatives of Christ in our world. I had hoped the Bishop would want to talk to me, apologize for what happened to me and pray with me. I had hoped that he would see the importance of seeking out other victims to help them heal. I had hoped The Church would use this revelation to grow, be open and reach out to people in pain. I had hoped they would see this as an opportunity to show the world what Christians stand for and that we do not compromise our values. I think a reasonable response would be to announce it to the world that as a community of faith we are going to fight until not one more child is made to suffer in this way again. And we will work to make amends in every way we can to those who have suffered under our past negligence.

Just as those things did not happen, I am not willing to just go quietly away. I will shout to the world what The Church did and did not do and hope that in time people will start to understand. It is time to take the yoke of shame off victims and their families and place it where it belongs, on the perpetrators, the system and people who protect them.

It is to this end I go forward, and dedicate my efforts to Austin, Brady, Harper, Lily, Daisy and Jack. May they grow up in a world free of abuse from trusted adults.

Amen

Chapter 6

coming out

What a surreal week. We went to Portland over the weekend and met with an attorney on Monday afternoon. That was every bit as hard as seeing the Inquisitors who came to the house, perhaps harder because it was in an unfamiliar place. I told him the story of my abuse and recovery to date.. The attorney said we had a very strong case. He offered that, in addition to asking for money and an apology, we could ask for policy changes in The Church's way of handling these problems.

I don't really like going to an attorney, but I don't know any other way to equalize the power differential between "The Church" and me. The money represents two things for me. First, it is some compensation for the damage to my life and my family, and second it serves as a bold demand for institutional change. I could ask The Church to proactively educate about the issue and address prevention. I think that's what I want to spend my upcoming time on.

Easier Without You

I let the secret out
I told on you
My family knows
The church knows
The court knows
I know
I emptied my gut of your poison
Finally got you out of my body
I gave up the secret elephant
I spent my life protecting

Now I have to heal myself
I quit drinking
I quit drugs…mostly
Clean and straight for 30 days
The first time in 40 years
The world looks different
I feel different
Not better yet
Just different
Empty actually
Everything I have spent emotional energy on is gone
Blank slate
Most reaction I can get
Is gospel music
My sis says it's slave music
Music to free the soul
And I been a slave all these years
'cause of your evil
I think she's right
The music stimulates my spirit
I need more
Now I gotta go lookin' for meaning
Gotta go find fun
Gotta learn new ways to love
Wanta learn to touch others
I'm at the bottom lookin' up
Gotta lot of learnin' to do
Gonna be hard
Easier though without you

We saw our good friends in Portland and had thought of telling them what was going on, but it didn't feel right. I'm not sure how to tell people who are close. I'm thinking they probably don't want to know and would have difficulty understanding. I still haven't said anything to one of my sisters. I *know* she would rather not know. I cannot see a good way to deal with this except to just tell them. I think this will be in the paper next week so I don't have much time. I just had the thought that I might talk to my brother-in-law instead of my sister. He would be easier to talk to, as she always wanted to stick her head in the sand when we were kids. It seems like every step of this process leads me to a new arena with its own set of problems that force me into new territory and, I hope, growth. *Sounds* good, but in this case growth is *extremely* difficult.

What a difference a few hours makes. I sent emails with a full explanation to two very close friends and my sister. One friend called me after reading it. She was horrified by what had happened to me and very impressed with my courage to do something about it. She seemed to fully understand all the emotions and ramifications. She could not have been more supportive. The other friend sent me an email that was without question the nicest and most complimentary letter I have ever received. Both said the one thing I have heard from everyone who has known me well: "This explains a lot."

My sister who is four years older than me, just called back and was sobbing. Her empathy was so comforting. She said she wished she could go back in time and help me. She also said mom would have stopped at nothing to right the wrong.

I told her I was scared to tell her because she never wanted to be involved in any controversy. She said that it was one thing to be a Pollyanna about things that didn't matter, but this matters and she needs to know it. Then my brother-in-law got on the phone and asked if he could pray with me. I said yes. As uncomfortable as that would normally make me, somehow it seemed appropriate and made me feel loved. I know there are lots of other victims out there that would not get this kind of reaction. I want to remember how fortunate I am to have the support of my family and friends.

The suit was filed yesterday. My attorney sent me a copy of the press release he put out today. It was good. Later in the week my counselor asked me to write what *I* would want a press release to say. Talk about a tough assignment. I would start with the piece I wrote, *Secrets and Lies*. I would want the release to reveal how even though I didn't keep the abuse in my conscious mind, it affected everything I did and how I did it, until I made the break and began to deal with it.

I am lucky. I have an excellent counselor, a loving family and caring friends. In confronting what had happened to me, I've had to give up control and what I probably thought was power. Let it all go. In doing so, I am finding a strength and faith that feels as powerful and blinding as the sun. In fact, while meditating the other day I was picturing the cross with Jesus on it, and the words "I Am." After a while Jesus was gone; the Son had become the sun—I saw an empty cross, the sun behind it and the words "I Am." The clear, basic imagery moved me profoundly. The strength we need is all around us if we just look and trust. I am finding new perspectives everywhere.

It turns out *The Oregonian* did not publish the attorney's press release. Apparently child sex abuse by a well-known pastor at a large prominent church many years ago isn't too newsworthy. It seems to me that every case of child sexual abuse should be newsworthy. They did talk about it at my old church (scene of the crime) on the following Sunday though.

The Church's Response

It is with great sadness
That I report a serious matter!
A multimillion-dollar lawsuit
Against OUR church!
A man CLAIMS
To have been sexually abused
Forty years ago
By a clergy here
Neither is part of us anymore
The Clergy surrendered his credentials
Following procedures
Outlined in our Church Discipline
Our Church Law
After hearing of the suit
Our Board of Trustees
Engaged an attorney
We are preparing
To give an *appropriate* response
To the *legal* issue

In this media-saturated day
You may hear reports
Designed to stir emotions
That's unfortunate
But a reality we live with

We abhor actions that abuse
The sacred trust of pastoral leaders
And cause others to suffer
We are now committed
To creating safety and security

As people of faith
We believe
It is important
To lift this man
And anyone suffering abuse
In our prayers.
Now for silent reflection
Then my colleague Dr. John will lead us in prayer

What I Heard

Hey everybody, listen up
We are being sued
For millions of our hard-earned money
A Man claims
Sexual abuse
By a minister here
You're not going to believe this part
FORTY years ago

I understand the man
His parents and sisters
His aunt and cousins
Attended, supported and were leaders
In this church from the 1930s to the 1970s

But really
They don't even attend here anymore
Now I should mention
The abuse was verified
By admission.
Oh, and we did follow church law of course,
With regard to procedure.
What does this man expect of us?

On your behalf
The Trustees
Hired the very same attorney
That represented
The Catholic Archdiocese
Against hundreds of men
CLAIMING sexual abuse
At the hands of local priests

We felt he would be the best person
To handle this *legal* situation.
You know,
Protect our *ass*ets
And he is very experienced
In dealing with these victims
Now I have to tell you
It makes me sick
But the media
Will probably try to hype this up
Trying to get people all worked up
Over an old case
Of child sex abuse
But that's a reality
We must live with

On both a practical and an intellectual level
We don't want our pastors
Abusing parishioners

We want you to feel safe coming
   to church

Never mind that a boy
Was sexually assaulted
By the minister here
Dozens of times
Over a period of years
In the office now occupied
By our very own Dr. John

And ladies I don't want you
Thinking about what this man
Claims happened to him
As a 16-year-old boy
In the dressing room
In our Narthex
That you use for preparations
For weddings and the like
(You know he could be making
Some of this up)

Because we are Christians
I think it is important
To pray for this man
And other victims
Let us silently reflect

What I Wanted to Hear

Fellow Christians
It is with great sadness
That I report to you
A matter so serious
That it brings me
To my knees
In sorrowful prayer

A fellow Christian
Has come forward to report
That he was sexually abused
And mentally tortured
By the minister here
When he was a teenager.
I cannot imagine the strength
It must have taken
For him to speak up

As is often the case
This man has lived with
And been impacted
By this
Every day
Year in, year out
Never telling a soul
Not even admitting it to himself

The self-admitted pedophile
Has had his license revoked by the Bishop
We will talk of this in every congregation
To send the same message that Christ did.
We will have zero tolerance
For anyone harming our children

The man has filed a lawsuit
Asking for money.
Obviously he feels he has been damaged
By what happened to him within these walls
And he wants us to take responsibility for our part in that.
So be it
The Trustees and I will work
To resolve the legal portion of this
Based on the values
We speak of
On Sunday mornings

From this very pulpit
And properly compensate
This man for the pain and suffering
He endured under our watch
And in Christ's own name

What you hear about this
In the news media
May be sensational and lopsided
But it cannot possibly come close
To the shame I feel today

I ask for your support
To do what we must
To rectify this horrible wrong

Let us pray
Dear Lord God
Help us to find a way
To make right
The things that happened here
In your name and ours.

Crimes so awful
As to make us
Not want to speak of them
Yet we must
If we are to make a difference

Grant us the courage
This man found to come forward
To seek Your Truth and Justice.
We commit this day
That we will not rest
Until all your children are safe
From this illness
That is so pervasive in our world
We believe we must find

The strength and compassion
To protect all those who come here
Seeking love and understanding.
May Your Grace become
A reality for us all
In a world where our children
Can feel safe from intentional harm
Amen

Chapter 7

the legal system

Now the real fun starts, discovery they call it. The Church's attorney's asked me to turn over every picture I have of myself over the period of abuse, my marriage license, all my tax returns for the last 10 years, records of any real estate my wife and I own, and other personal documents. As if that wasn't bad enough. Then they ask for:

- any books I had read on the subject of abuse,
- any websites I had visited regarding abuse,
- anything I had written in the form of journals (for my entire life),
- any emails I had written or written to me mentioning my abuse,
- and finally (the coup de grace!) a mirror copy of my computer's hard drive.

What the Church's attorneys call "discovery", my counselor calls *revictimization*. The attempted intimidation was unbelievable. Who's the criminal here? I went crazy. I felt like I was being raped. My anxiety went to the moon. My counselor actually talked to the attorneys' office and asked them to back off for my sanity.

In the end we rejected some of the items and I flatly refused to give them a copy of my computer.

Flow Baby Flow

My wife and children have kidded me for years
Go with the flow dad
Little did they know
Nor did I
That flow was impossible for me

Sorry kids
My word must be law
Don't question it
I must stay strong
Always keep my eye on the road
Look neither left nor right
Rarely glance in the rearview mirror
Bend not
Rigidity equals strength
Don't you realize
I'm trying to hold this together
If I question anything
I may have to question everything

Now the very source of the fear
Broken trust
And stolen soul
The Church—is at it again

When they have been given an opportunity
To attempt to repair and seek forgiveness
They come with new invasions
Poking, prodding,
Accusing the victim
Stripping me naked
Just like before.
At the same time
They give my abuser
"A new role in the church"

They invade my home
As well as my soul
I guess they find it easier
To blame the victim
Than to take responsibility

I have finally looked in my rearview mirror
Faced the monsters there
The monsters of my youth are gone now
But new ones come
This time I find
My best option is flow
It seems paradoxical
That the original source of my rigid race through life
Has come back to teach me a better way
Ruin me once
Shame on you
Ruin me twice
Shame on me

I will allow the evil
That is emanating
From the bell towers
Of Corporate Christianity
To wash over me
I will bend in the wind
Of their foul breath
I will learn to be strong like a bow
Not like a granite column
Their evil will find
No fuel to set ablaze in me
Or my home
I will finally learn Flow
Dear God I must
To retain my sanity

Maybe we have a breakthrough. The Bishop's attorney wants to meet me informally. My attorney thinks that after he meets me, they may want to work things out amicably. Sounds great to me. Put an end to this insanity. So, off to Portland I go, scared, nervous, and hopeful.

Christian Loving Care

Went to Portland for an attorneys' meeting
I prepared for two weeks
I was ready to show them who I was
And how my life had been turned upside-down
My guy told me to show how successful I was
How I'm not a flake
Don't show 'em the touchy-feely stuff.
But that's where I'm at!
That's the part I lost being a victim
I'm working on learning to touch and feel again

Then the bishop's guy says to me
What is your culpability in this affair
What?
There was no "affair" from my way of thinking
Unless you call adulation an affair
And culpability means what did I do to make the
        preacher want me
Kind of like askin' the rape victim what she was wearin'
"Did you smile funny-like?"
Bastards try to make the victim look like they did
        somethin' wrong
Then he wants to know how long 'til I'm well
Good question
How long does it take recover lost spirit and grace?
For the bishop's man the sooner the better
It's a liability thing you know
My answer is probably never

Then they give me a letter from the bishop
Tells me he's saddened by this
"Incident of sexual misconduct"
He offers the opportunity to meet with him
So he can be pastoral with me
My guy is real impressed

Wow
I feel better already
This is the boss of the guy whose attorney
Just asked me what my culpability was
And then asked repeatedly when I would be done
        with recovery
I guess I should be grateful
For all this Christian loving care

   I should mention that this whole meeting was conducted with great civility
and manners. Needless to say, I was more than disappointed. This "shortcut" was
obviously going nowhere. These people were all about denial, limiting exposure
and liability. Back to more "discovery." What an innocent and enlightening
sounding word. I think it should be officially changed to colonoscopy, but I
guess that's already been taken.

Chapter 8

the struggle continues

When I was in my twenties, a man I knew and respected once told me that sarcasm was unbecoming in a person as young as I was. Unfortunately, the sarcasm has only grown over the years. Due to the extremity of my denial, it was the trait that got fed the most. The process continues as does my struggle.

Never Give Up

Having a drink
Or gettin' a bowl
Seems like quitting
Giving up
Accepting defeat
That's not what I want
Not what I'm about anymore
So be strong
Lean on anybody
Just don't quit on me
That's so easy to write
Why is it so hard to do?

When the anxiety or frustration builds
Nothing else hits home
Like a shot or a couple of puffs
Damn I hate that
Don't you understand
That's not what I want to do
I want to let the feelings flow out of me

Not get stuck inside
Where I can't get at them

I want to feel good in an hour
I want to wake up with a clear head
And a smile in my mind
Not headed to the bathroom
Turning on the fan
Getting a lift
From my drug of choice
Please God help me be strong

In addition to learning and growing from weekly counseling, I have found a church to help strengthen me and open my soul. It has been a huge help to my recovery. I am not really socializing there, but the sermons and music almost always hit home. It gives my spirit a lift and I am more focused when I leave. I seem to do most of my writing either after counseling or church. Interestingly, the other victims I have come to know also seem to have a strong church life or faith in a higher power to help them overcome the impossible weight of abuse.

Yesterday

I went to church yesterday morning
The music made me sad
I left feeling loss
An old man sitting in the back
Got up and followed me out
He put his hands on my shoulders
And looked me in the eye
He asked what was wrong
I told him I was in pain
He told me to take care of myself
Take care of me
And he held me there a minute
I was so moved by his love I cried

That's not what you did Ron is it?
Right after you touched my shoulders
You put your hands down my pants
I think I'm going to replace the memory of you
With the memory of the old man

When I got home I put on gospel music
I went diggin' in my cellar
I wandered through all those dark corners
I opened up my loneliness
I visited anger, hurt, betrayal, even death
I was numb
Then I found something unexpected
My soul
Hidden away for all these years

I cried over lost joy
I sobbed for hours as I thought of your theft
I got food poisoning from leftover Chinese food
As the poison literally flowed from my body
I thought of your poison flowing out of me
Yours, not mine

I give back what is yours
I have wanted you out of my life for so long
Your chains no longer hold me
And now I'm reclaiming my soul

Every step of the way, as I discover more about myself and the impact of abuse on my life, I want others to hear and really "get it." I want them to see that child sex abuse changes a person in a way that you can't change back. Later I learn this will take a lifetime and some people will never understand how heinous this crime really is.

Position Statement

I am moving from victim
To survivor
From hardliner to balanced
My foundation is growing
Now when I consciously say
I will no longer be a victim
It comes from inner strength
And confidence, not from fear

"The Church" is working
To keep me a victim
I respectfully decline

I will not allow
This process to weaken me
Victimize me
All over again
I will protect myself
I will set firm limits
I have the power of the universe
And Christ at my side
Truth lights my path

I will expose their evil
Just as I know Jesus
Would rage at the corruption
And destruction of His Children
Paradox or double speak
It's all the same in His eyes
Evil
And the walls come tumbling down

One of my biggest issues has been lack of trust. My greatest strength has been my faith. If I am going to fully recover I need to learn to trust people. Easier said than done. I have trouble even following the logic. This one isn't going to happen overnight.

Trust-Faith

Does faith mean I don't have to control everything
Or is that trust?
It seems silly to say that I trust there is a God
Yet I have faith there is a higher power
Does it seem odd to anyone else
That I find it easier to have faith
Than to trust?
You see my faith can't fail me
Because there is no countering data
My parameters won't allow it

Yet I have experienced countless failures in trust
Perhaps when my trust was broken
By the person closest to me
I closed the door
And have never opened it more than a crack
Never opened it enough for anyone
To get more than an arm or leg through
To be honest I don't even know what trust feels like
Maybe I could use my faith
To begin to learn to trust people again
Do you suppose that would work?

Chapter 9

things that count

Once again I find my soul and mind opened at church. Even though I do not consider myself a "churchie" it seems to be a source of constant stimulation.

Talents

At church today
They read the story about
God giving out talents
As in coin, cashola
The ones that invested the cash
And made more
Were the good guys
The one that was fearful
And buried his
So he wouldn't lose it
Got raked over the coals by God
And sent away
It's not how much you have that counts
It's what you do with what you have

I never had trouble sharing the cash
Mom said we should share what we have
So I did
It wasn't risky
It was what we were supposed to do
I got stopped when it came to sharing myself
My personal talents

As a child I got burned
For sharing me
It re-formed me
Kinda like a plastic toy
That gets too close to a fire
It gets all melted and bent
And then hardens all twisted
As it cools

I let it change me for life
Locked up real tight
Mom was gone by 22
Never knew a real teacher again
To help me past the hurt

I had a lot of talent to work with
But I kept it buried for the most part
I'd call that sin
Kinda like in traffic court
Plead guilty with an explanation
And hope the judge lowers the fine
I have let countless needs of others
That were obvious to me
Float right by
Without giving even a little
Of what I was capable of
May the Universe forgive me
The time has come to wake up
Break out of my self-imposed cage
Take off my mask
Dig out what has been buried
Put my fear in the hole
And leave it behind
Open up my wings
And learn to fly again
Let my talents see the light of day
And see what grows
Amen

My lack of vision regarding where this process will take me is continuously amazing. At the beginning I never expected to report this. I *never* would have imagined actually filing a lawsuit. Get off alcohol and drugs? *Me?* No way. I have changed in ways I never could have foreseen. Just like the changing of the seasons, things seem to happen in a natural order. They don't happen until I'm ready for them or ready to hear it.

In God We Trust

Birthdays are not a joyous occasion to me
December 21
Is a lousy time to have a birthday
Which gifts under the tree
Are to be opened four days early?
Oops, the present that goes with those batteries,
Has to wait four days

It's been a very tough year
So this year I went to church
On my naming day
Didn't want to be there
Not one Christmas carol I knew
In the pastoral prayer before the sermon
The preacher asks that we open our ears
To hear what we need from the Word
Okay mom, I remember
You told me that every Sunday morning as a
        teenager
Go to church
Listen
You will always
Find something of value
Hearing that I knew
There was a good reason
To be in church today
But I sure didn't know what it was

And then it came
The very end of the sermon
As soon as I heard it
I knew it was my message that day
The miracle of Mary
Wasn't that she conceived
But rather that she trusted
Okay a teenage girl has a dream
It tells her she will have a baby
The baby is the Son of God
Now go get married
Right
Amazingly she believed it
No proof necessary
Just trust in the unknown
Easier said than done

Sounds simple
But that was it
My recent aimless drift on the ocean
And continuing efforts to stuff
A five-pound sleeping bag
Into a three-pound cover
Have been the product
Of trying too hard
And thinking too much
Trying to make sense of it all
Still wanting to control
What I cannot.
Instead of reason
I needed to trust
The God I had learned to love

When I get home the phone rings
My sister-in-law wants to come over
With birthday greetings
Can't say no, so okay

My nephew hands me a card he made
It's a thank you card
For all the things I do for him

Brings a tear to my eye
And I tell him
It's the nicest card I have ever gotten

Inside the card is a dollar bill
He says it's not to spend
He tells me about a movie he watched
The lawyer is trying to prove
There is a Santa Claus
It's not working

At the end of the movie
He takes a dollar bill
And tells the court that we put
"In God We Trust" on our money
But we have no proof there is a God
So Jack says that means
There probably is a Santa

And then my nephew
Turns the dollar over and I see
He has circled the words
"In God We Trust" in red
WOW
I am blown away
I tell him thank you
For the nice card
And confirming what the preacher said
Trust in God

I've thought about that
Several times a day for a week
Is that what those fanatics mean
When they say God spoke to them

Or called them?
I don't want to be one of *them*
But I gotta tell you
He spoke to me
As clearly as if He was in the room
Randy, trust Me
Quit drifting
Quit worrying
Keep doing what you know is right,
To the best of your ability

Keep open to new ideas and learning
Your life experiences will come into play
When the time is right
You will know what to do
Trust me Randy
Trust in God
Happy Birthday

That dollar bill with *In God We Trust* circled in red hangs in a frame over my computer as a constant reminder.

Chapter 10

something old, something new

It's Epiphany Sunday. On this, the one-year anniversary of my first meeting with The Church hierarchy, I reflect on my experiences. One might think that I brought all this on myself by expecting too much. Then, feeling unsatisfied, I contacted an attorney and filed a lawsuit. Why should I be surprised by the reaction I got from The Church? What's ironic to me at this point is that the real reason for my disillusionment is that I *believed what I learned in church*: peace, love, do unto others, protect of the rights of the individual. Institutions and corporations should not be allowed to run over the individual. I reacted to being a victim by adamantly defending my rights as I saw them.

Christians or Antichrist?

I suffered through years of abuse
At the hands of the preacher
I lived with it for decades
I survived months of psychotherapy
I had the strength and faith
To beat my addictions
I still sought comfort in God's house

Not until I sought Justice
From The Church
Did I find the antichrist
Instead of reaching out with love
And asking for forgiveness
They struck out with
Fists and kicks

Accusations and attacks
They had their lawyers do the fighting
While they strutted their piousness
And hid behind their collective robes
One hand held the Bible
The other a check for the lawyers

I guess I missed the Bible verses
Cover thine own ass
And, do the other guy
Before he does you
Praise Jesus
And pass the communion tray

As I look at my own life, I am beginning to take responsibility for things I would rather have put onto others (or not even recognized at all). My most important realization pertains to what kind of a parent and partner I have actually been, which is not at all what I have stored as memories. My next realization involves how I related to others in general. Being a perfectionist, I have always looked at life experiences as an opportunity to improve. That's what I was taught. Hmmm, maybe there is a reason people quickly tire of being around me.

It Don't Take No Talent to be a Critic

It's so easy to find fault
Other people's shortcomings
Are as easy to spot
As a crooked picture on the wall
Are you going out looking like that?
Can you believe how nasty she was?
I'm sure you did the best you could
What a horse's ass
Did you see how much he drank?
Are you going to leave that there?
Bad night?

Did you see the gap in that trim?
You know that beam isn't level
What did you say?
Getting a haircut soon?
You must be tone deaf
Want a mint?
Plug up the toilet *again*?
Learn to drive, asshole

Seems like maybe
Every time we say these things
We hurt ourselves
As well as the people
We say them about
Kinda like we bring the whole world down
No skill involved
Just shoot at will

I been thinkin'
Maybe the real talent
Is in sayin' something nice
I ain't kiddin'
If I say somethin'
That makes you feel good
Then you smile
That makes me smile
And maybe we make
The world a little better place

I know this means
I been wasting my life
With my witty jabs
And clever observations
To help make *you* a better person
Funny, I thought you would take it better

I never found much acceptance
Being sincere

I always cared,
Just seemed to get further with sarcasm
I want to try a different way
Better late than never
Gonna take notice of what is right
Not what's wrong

Just think how much more
We could accomplish in life
If we felt better about ourselves
And each other
I want to fill my world
With good thoughts
Want to share them with you too

On one of my trips to Portland I met an old friend for lunch. He told me a story about his cousin and her abuse. I had met her a few times over the years and knew she had some problems, but I never knew why. I was so moved by that when I came home I felt the need to tell Penny's story. Unfortunately her story is not rare and happens all too often. I hope you don't mind I am sharing it in my book Penny. It is with the greatest respect that I speak of your life and death that others might see through your eyes.

Oh Penny

I'm so sorry for the pain you suffered
All alone
It's not the kind of pain you share
When Mark first told me about you
I wanted to kill somebody
He said that your older sister
Tried to report
What was happening to you at home
The same thing that happened to her before you
She wanted to get you out of there

Then it didn't happen
It was just too much for two young victims to pull off
How do you stand up against mom and dad

The things you have to admit not only to yourselves
But say out loud to the world
Are just too horrible to imagine
I don't know where strength like that comes from
So everybody went back to pretending
Pretending what was happening wasn't

As the years went by
Drugs flowed through your body and mind
Uppers, downers anything to get you through the long
        days and nights
To help you forget
And then the surgeries started
I'm told they counted in the dozens
Funny I would never have thought of literally trying
        to cut out the pain
But can see how that would make sense to you
Anything to try to get it out of your body
I'm not sure anybody that hasn't lived with this can
        understand
But I do
It's almost like having a Siamese twin attached to you
That nobody can see
And you pretend isn't there

But you have to adjust everything you do
To compensate for this overwhelming burden
That doesn't exist

 Your pain is finally gone
They said your heart stopped
I heard your family was relieved to know
That they identified what finally broke
How fortunate for them

To have something acceptable
To put in the "cause of death" blank

Mark asked me to go to your service with him
The preacher made it sound like you were a sinner
And a lost sheep
Maybe you would have some trouble at the pearly gates
I'm pretty sure he had no clue what he was talking about
The most vile sin on earth
To steal the soul of a child

Doesn't seem quite fair
That you were judged for their sins.

You are no more
I'll bet that Saint Peter himself will greet you with the
    greatest of fanfare
Or perhaps a simple foot washing
To cleanse away the sins of others
From your body and mind
To give you back the innocence and beauty
That was ripped from you as a child

I don't know how you bore it
For your 35 years
I want to yell it to the hills
The injustice you endured
The real cause of death
The pain was so bad
You couldn't take another breath
I grieve for you
And for those who still bear the burden of their secret
Goodbye my sister

Ever noticed how some people can never be satisfied? Always the critic, we know something is wrong. We just can't place it. The wrong, the discomfort is actually inside of us, but since we are blind to the problem, we look for the imbalance outside of ourselves. It must be out there somewhere because I can feel it. It feels like a déjà vu only it's more like déjà me.

Unease

Balance is simply unattainable
A person who was abused as a child
Goes to incredible extremes
To make the invisible go away
We don't know what it is
But somethin' just
Don't feel right

We are so miserable
That we project that unease
On all we see
Nothing is ever good enough
No matter how we try to make it right
We cannot be satisfied
It is almost as though
We need to create the same discomfort
In the outside world
That we feel on the inside
Or maybe it's just
That since we can't fix what's inside
We try to fix everything on the outside
Either way something always feels wrong

My addictions and my loneliness are the two issues that keep coming up over and over and over. Even though I am around family every day, I tend to keep my feelings to myself—a product of hiding for so many years. Since I stay so much in my own head, it had never occurred to me how this hiding impacts my wife and kids. Only now am I realizing that it is a form of selfishness to the extreme. Acting like a victim is a totally self-absorbed way to live. Originally I hid for safety, but now hiding has become my habitual comfort zone.

Lonely Satisfaction

I'm pissed
I'm embarrassed
As I struggle to kick my addictions
I find breaking the physical part doable
I'm good at it,
Most of the time
Alone for a few days
I find myself
Cooking meals and treats that I love
Mmmm… tastes good

Then I decide a day of relapse
Wouldn't be the end of the world
Besides what's wrong
With feeling good for a change
A little stimulation
For the emotions
Go to that place that feeds
My right brain needs
It's been my way
For a long, long time

I have been struggling
With being out
In that other world
That public place
Where it feels strange
And a little bit scary
Better to be polite
Than honest

My self-indulgent weekend
Provided me a new perspective
My time alone was
To nurture myself.

I'm sad to say
I feel more comfort
In my private world
I hide my need for love
And acceptance around others
I honor it when I am alone
I won't let others love me
But my need drives me
To seek fulfillment
In food and drugs
By myself

May I find the strength
To be honest with myself
And with loved ones
To ask for what I need
May I find satisfaction
In relationships with others
Rather than in solitude
If I risk telling you mine
You might share your needs as well
We both get what we need
Then maybe we can share
What they call reciprocal love

Chapter 11

seeking understanding

As the day of my deposition draws closer, I feel both fear and a strong need to be understood as a victim/survivor. So far the entire process with The Church, my friends and family, has left me feeling unsatisfied. I want people to immerse themselves in what it is like to be a victim. I know that is unreasonable and yet it is how I feel.

What's the Big Deal?

When I was young
My dream was to attend
Prescott College
A new alternative school in Arizona
It didn't happen
It didn't even come close

My life was so controlled
By my mentor/ abuser
That everyone else
Was shut out
Anyone who might have helped me on my path
Including my parents
Had ceased to be part of my life
He saw to that.
The abuse syndrome
Saw to that.
Keep the secret
Trust no one

So when I broke
With my mentor/abuser
Age 18
I had no one.
Mom died 3 years later
Dad was drunk
No support system
Alone
It's no wonder my life
Just started meandering
Like George Harrison says
"If you don't know where you're goin'
Any road will take you there"

You may ask
What's the big deal
Things happen to everyone
Move on
Right?

I lived for years without a direction
No plan
No past
No future
Do the best you can
Don't let anyone get the upper hand on you
That's life
Suck it up and deal
Keep everyone at a distance
Move when things get tight
Show no weakness
Right or wrong
Make sure no one gets close enough
To hurt
Or to help.
My dreams
My hopes

My heart
My soul
They never happened
Crushed before they started
Life without a rudder
Destroyed by corrupt power

So what's the big deal
Right?

All of us, to differing degrees, hide aspects of ourselves from the rest of the world. Those of us who have experienced severe trauma, especially as children, probably tend to keep more hidden because we are unable to face ourselves, let alone others.

Seeking Understanding

Most of us
Have an inner self
And an outer self
The inner self is where
We keep our hopes and dreams
Our feelings and emotions
We evaluate and process
Our relationship to
The outside world

The outer self
Is the one
Who meets and greets others
Who goes to work
The one who goes on dates
Gets married
And raises children

Some people
Seem to be the same
Inside and out

We say of them
"What you see is what you get"

A victim of abuse
Who has not dealt with it
Will never be that transparent
How could he? How could she?
And still maintain the secret

Even saying aloud
"I was a victim"
Falls way short
Of saying what that
Means to them

Most who have been sexually abused
By a loved one
Lock away our inner selves
In a state of fear and confusion
And take it to our graves
Never to see the light of day

Those of us
Who choose to tell our story
Seeking truth and justice
Rarely find the
Understanding we seek
In the end
We find
That must come from within

Chapter 12

deposition

The timing of my deposition, which I had been told, could last eight hours or more, works to my advantage. It's difficult to schedule a bunch of lawyers together before one in the afternoon, so I have time to gather myself. At 11:30, I park at my attorney's office. I have time to walk along the Willamette River, listen to my music and look across at Kaiser Hospital where my oldest daughter was born. That was so cool—scary but cool. We were 22 at the time and still babies ourselves. It helps ground me to think of my family. Even though my abuse took place in this city, so did many other major events in my life.

At noon I go into the office, as pre-arranged, to get last-minute instructions from my attorney. Keep answers short. Do not volunteer *anything*. Do not expound. The best answers are yes, no and I don't recall. This is *not* the time to tell your story. That comes when we get a jury. Be honest. They will try to trip you up by asking the same question differently. The best way to not get confused is to just tell the truth. He closes by telling me the opposing attorney can ask *anything* he wants (there is no judge to stop him) and my attorney cannot say a word. If things get desperate, he can call for a break so we can go outside the room and talk. This is not quite what I envisioned. I can't even bring in my tablet, where I had written the twenty-third Psalm and the names of friends and family who would be with me in spirit. I feel completely *alone* cut off from the outside world, which I'm pretty sure is the intent.

The week before, my counselor had asked me to visualize what would help me feel safe in a potentially hostile setting. I came up with a suit of armor. The lawyers couldn't get to me and I could always lower the face guard so they couldn't even see me. We had discussed the setting's power differential and its similarity to being abused and made to feel vulnerable. *Revictimization* was her term for it. Unfortunately I am sure that this process alone would keep some victims from coming forward.

When I walk into the room I am overwhelmed. I expect to see a couple of Church attorneys and my attorney, but all ten of the seats at the conference table are taken. They brought everybody they could find—at least four attorneys, the Bishop, an accountant or two and a court reporter. Gang rape is the term that comes to mind, except only one of their attorneys could play the role of Inquisitor. He does the job while the others watch. His questions range from was I sexually active in high school (outside of the abuse of course!), to hadn't I lived a pretty successful life? What do I really have complain about? He doesn't ask many questions about the abuse itself. Primarily, he wants everybody to see what a great life I've had. He had obviously talked to people I had worked with in the past and they confirmed his game plan (because they all knew me so well of course).

This interrogation is carried out with more smiles and "nicey-nice" than you could possibly imagine. Four plus hours later, one of the "spectator" attorneys has another appointment to go to, so our little gathering comes to an abrupt end. Peaches and Cream (aka interrogator) puts me on notice that he is not yet done questioning me, and depending on how things go, he would need another appointment to finish.

Afterwards, my attorney tells me I did an excellent job, as good as he has seen. Imagine the emotional state of someone who has been badgered for over four hours with ten other people watching. I feel—catatonic, drained and empty.

I would like to ask every attorney and judge: Isn't there any way to change this system to make it easier on the victim? Perhaps limit the interrogation parameters or allow an advocate (possibly appointed by the court) to sit beside *the accused*?

I know of a movement in legal circles called Collaborative Family Law. The intent, as I understand it, is to help people move through the difficult process of divorce as amicably as possible, without the added pain of embittered conflict. How much better it would be if, in legal actions involving abuse, institutions offered to hire Collaborative Attorneys and resolve these cases outside of the courts. It would be less costly and less painful for everyone involved.

The Time Has Come

Lawyers and Legislators
Bishops and Churches
School districts and Principals
Beware the evil you defend

Whether or not
You perceive abusers as monsters
I can assure you
Their behavior
And its results
Are monstrous
Hundreds of years ago
It was common
In some cultures
To perform
Human sacrifice
The thought repulses us now
How could people allow it?
It occurs today
In the form of
Child sexual abuse
Our government
And each of us
Allow it to happen
By our inaction

This destruction
Of life, motivation and purpose
Could not be more complete
Than if you drained
The blood of a child
And replaced it with
Fear, dread, mistrust
And loneliness

The sexual abuse of children
Has robbed our society
Of millions of potential teachers, leaders,
And contributors to a better world

The time has come
To quit allowing the system
To re-victimize the victims
Start prosecuting the pedophiles
No matter how much time has passed
Make abusers accountable
For the destruction they wreak

The time has come
To pull our collective head
Out of the sand
The time has come
To deal with that which we would not speak of
And we wish would go away on its own
But will not

The time has come to
Defend our children
Past, present and future
Fulfill our moral obligation
To those who are most vulnerable and valuable;
Our Children

Chapter 13

in society and the world

Love and Acceptance

The lawyers keep asking
What precipitated seeking counseling
After 40 years?
I keep saying
Something was missing
They say
You've done pretty well
Ya, I'm a good survivor
But survival
Is not the same thing as livin'
Survival alone
Is not enough for me
I need to LIVE
To be able to feel
To express a full range of emotions
And not be afraid to show who I am

We are social animals
We need the Love
And Acceptance of others
To be complete

A person sexually abused as a minor
Has virtually no hope
Of letting anybody
Close enough

To love
Or be loved
Safety must always come first

A normal human reaction to something unpleasant is to minimize it and put it behind us as quickly as we can. I certainly did this continuously before I became aware of being a victim. I recently met a policewoman who told me that, during morning briefings at the station, even other officers don't want to hear about her child abuse cases. If she tries to discuss these cases, someone invariably interrupts her and changes the subject. She said that juries also hate these cases. Such a strong tendency toward denial in police stations and courtrooms shows how embedded the barriers are to changing this culture of abuse. Each of us needs to take it upon ourselves to do what we can, where we can.

Let's Move On

Just read an article in the paper
A cop in Bend raised money to buy a camera
That takes pictures to show eye injury
In babies who have been physically abused
What a great thing!
Says it's tough to work those cases
People don't want to talk about it
And the kids can't
Or won't
They say the camera is really noninvasive
A way to find evidence of abuse

It's too bad there isn't a camera
To take a picture of the soul
So we could see evidence
Of sexual abuse
Unfortunately
It's an invisible epidemic
When we look at people
We don't see the predator

Kinda like the bugs we used to call no see-ums
Nobody can see 'em
And only the victim
Can feel the bite

We can't imagine coach Don, or pastor Jim,
Or John and Rosalie's family at church,
Or those sweet foster parents who take in homeless kids
Doing unspeakable things to children in their care
There isn't any real evidence, is there?
And look at all the good they do
Are you *sure* they did that?
I didn't think so
Let's move on

I have always reacted strongly when hearing about cases of abuse, but now that I have opened my own Pandora's box, I have become highly sensitized to things that constitute abuse. Forcing junior to be affectionate with Aunt Jane when he doesn't want to is not a message to give our children. It's like saying: "You don't have the right to protect your body; if someone older wants to touch or kiss you, you must let them." So many behaviors are on the fringe, or are predecessors to abuse: tickling a child to excess after he or she says "stop" or inappropriately teasing someone are forms of bullying.

Witnessing such behavior on a recent camping trip really upset me. As I watched this scene unfold my stomach tightened and by the end my fists were clenched and I wanted to either scream or run.

Little Sister

Sittin' in the campground
Watchin' the river flow by
Readin' a book
Couple o' families
Come to play in the water

Lots of yellin'
The Big Boy's role

Seems to be to dunk them all
Waters' freezin'
Moms are on the bank
Eggin' em on
First little girl victim
Is screamin'
But seems to be
Enjoyin' the attention

Once she gets wet
Big Boy goes after her little sister
'Bout nine or so

She stands on a log
That's layin' across the river
Holds on tight
For all she's worth
To a sapling
Growin' up out of the dead tree
Fightin' for her life

Big Boy can't get her loose
Another bro comes to help
She's screamin good an' loud now
Cryin' too
Moms still rootin' for the boys
My stomach's in a knot now
After bout five minutes
They break her free
Into the water she goes
She just stands there
Lays her head on the log
And sobs into that dead old tree
Boys go to the bank
Guess they need a rest
After finishing their big job

Mom's shouting
"Crybaby!
'Fraid of a little water!
Scaredy-cat"

The FUN was over
They packed up
Walked back down the road
Little sister bout 20 feet behind
Walkin' with her head down
As they walked out o' sight
I could hear mom's taunts
"Scaredy-cat
Fraid of a little water
Crybaby
Spoil everybody's fun"

I am continually surprised at the impact the abuse has had on the rest of my life. I don't want to blame it for all my problems and issues, but I can't ignore the connection. It frequently determines what I will or won't do.

The Good Old Times

Got a call about my 40-year class reunion
Gawd there's some major anxiety
Wanted to hear about it
But wouldn't consider going

I feel ashamed
Of the immature mistakes
I made when I was young
Young-immature
Imagine that!
But there it is
Shame
Shame of childhood?

Partly, but there's more
Shame about what happened to me
About being a victim
As though I was responsible
And people know it
I can feel it
So I can't go back
Even though they don't really know
The shame stops me
Like a roadblock
Victims can't look back
So we take one day at a time
Surviving they call it
Makes ya tough
Makes ya strong
Doesn't make you feel good
Doesn't make you happy

There's another step out there
It's called recovery
Been doin' it for two years now
Clean and sober

Relationships are better
Life is better
But I still can't go back
Class reunions aren't for victims
The "Good Old Times"
Just don't seem so good

Chapter 14

branching out

Although I had reached a point in my therapy where I thought I was coping well intellectually, somehow I realized I was holding my trauma in physically and needed help in releasing it. The emotional impact of abuse is imprinted on the body, which needs therapy as well. I was referred to a Body Talk practitioner who also happened to be a chiropractor. I am not going to try to explain the process here, but I will tell you it did produce results.

The Woo-Woo Doctor

Told my counselor
My mind's better
Now I need
To get it out of my body
She sent me to a woo-woo doctor
Who calls it "Body Talk"
She asks my body questions
And evidently it answers.
Okay.
First time I go
She tells me I was choked
Couldn't express myself
Happened before I was three
Says it was my dad.
Makes sense to me
Next time she tells me
My dad had a bad temper

And was mad a lot
Duh
Then she says I felt his anger
When I was in the womb
My body tells her
It was 75 percent of the time

Never liked my dad much
So this all just confirmed
It started a lot earlier
Than I was aware

Now I'm not sure
How all this works
But I gotta tell ya
The things she says
Ring true.
I'm wiped out when I leave
And I sleep like a rock
For a few days afterward
Now the third time I go
I get talkin' 'bout my liver
Regular Doc says it ain't so good
She says with work
It can get better

Then she starts her woo-woo stuff
She tells me
I'm holdin' fear in there
Fear from when the good Reverend
Was abusin' me
Fear like what if I told
How would I do it?
Who would I tell?
She told me to go back
And imagine telling somebody
Let it go

Even after two years of therapy
This was new territory for me
I lay on that table
And tried to imagine telling someone
I really did
But I couldn't
Who would I tell?
What would happen?
In the first place
He was my Teacher
I looked up to Him
He was a man of God
He was an Icon
People followed Him
Everybody knew how gifted He was
Folks competed
Just to get His attention
He was Holy
He could not possibly be bad
He couldn't be evil.
Of this I am sure

I have come to the conclusion
There was no way
I could have reported
What He did to me at the time
Reason dictates
That it would
Take decades
To be able to tell what he did

And it's not like I figured out
Something was wrong with him.
I finally realized in my fifties
Something was wrong with *me*
With *my life*

And after talking
To a counselor
For a few months,
I finally figured out it was *him* not me
Then it took me
Another six months
In therapy
To decide
To finally tell someone

Although I have not continued these treatments, I do think they helped. Body Talk advocates believe every one of our cells has complete memory. As I have continued my journey, I am finding that many survivors report physical manifestations of their abuse, some very dramatic; surgeries and illnesses that come out of nowhere, but are real just the same.

Chapter 15

getting at the core

At the core of my recovery, underneath all the other issues, is shame. I suspect this is true for every child victim. Mental health experts say that shame underlies most family secrets and only when we address the secrets can we begin to heal. When you tell the secret it loses it's power.

Shame, Shame, Shame

Shame for not telling
If someone commits a crime against you
You are supposed to report it
Admit you were duped
Turn 'em in
So they don't trick somebody else
Unmanly to admit
To being a victim
I didn't
I couldn't

Shame for not stopping it
A boy's s'posed to be able
To take care of himself

If he can't
He ain't a man
Wimp
Puss

And then the worst of all
Shame for it feeling good
I'm pretty sure
That makes me
A perv or a sicko too
Some folks'd say
"He got what he deserved"
A teen in the throws of puberty
Hormones raging
Someone older (and wiser?)
Touches your private parts
Your eyes are closed
'Cause on one hand you don't want to be there
On the other it feels good

How do you store that memory?
You lock it away as tight as you can
And cover it in a shroud of shame
Unbearable shame
I understand it now,
Intellectually
But it still embarrasses me
To admit it today
Society attaches shame
To sexual abuse of children
It slides right off the perpetrator
And finds a home
In the heart and mind
Of the victim

On my road
As I tell my truth
At first the shame
Takes my breath away
Gradually
It's lessening its grip on me

I need to emphasize what a horrible dichotomy this is. An adult sexually touches a pubescent boy. The boy is unable to stop the purely physical reaction of arousal, and he gets this "feel good" sensation, but it comes from a place he knows is wrong. Inside him, it's like two trains colliding head-on. What is supposed to feel good now makes him feel bad, bad about himself. A young person cannot understand this without professional help, and he finds it virtually impossible to have a healthy attitude about sex and sexuality. Lines that are made clear to most people are blurred or nonexistent to victims of child sexual abuse.

When you take away a person's self-esteem, you invalidate him or her. The victim is left with the impossible task of figuring out how to go forward with the injury. How does he or she save face, or do they even try?

I guess we all try; some are just better at faking it.

The Power of No

Yes and no
Yes I will.
No I won't.
Two simple phrases
Express my willingness
Or unwillingness
To participate
I choose
We all choose

When as children
We are psychologically forced
To take part in behavior
We neither choose nor understand
Our right
To say no is taken away
Normal relational boundaries
Are destroyed.
Abuse becomes confused with love

Physical pain and inappropriateness
Are confused with sex

Love means
Doing whatever
You are told
And keeping it a secret
Sex with virtually anyone
Is acceptable.
Or it is not
Acceptable at all.

Whichever way
Something is wrong
Something is nasty about it
And I am probably the cause

By taking away my right to say no
I lose control over my life
So I react
To protect myself
Either I say yes
When I would like to say no
Or I adamantly
Say no whenever I feel threatened.
I may find protection
In one or the other
But hiding is still hiding

Both paths create loneliness
Both paths require secrecy
Both paths are denial
Of what we are feeling
And what is real

For me, a major challenge is learning to set appropriate boundaries in my relationships. I find I feel a personal threat from men of power. I see them as infringing on my personal space and wanting to dominate the air space as well. I am affronted and angry. How do I comfortably protect my space without being an ass? I must remember that I have new tools now that I did not have earlier in life, or as an adolescent. And I need to rid myself of my resentment and fear and be confident in using my adult tools.

Power

Power = Corruption
Men have Power
Men assume Power
Men abuse Power
Arrogant men abuse their assumed Power
Men assume entitlement to Power
Men use assumed Power,
With no regard to those it impacts
Some men use Power to abuse
They think it demonstrates their Superiority
These tenets describe a bully culture

We live in a bully culture
It is the basis for abuse of all kinds
It starts in preschool
It takes on an unusual cruelty in High School
Then continues into family life
It permeates politics
As well as the workplace

We need to teach
At home and at school
That it is wrong
For anyone
To use force
Over another human being
So we may finally
Begin to create
A culture of equality
And fairness to all

Idealistic?
You bet
And why not?

Chapter 16

family of origin

By intimating that my parents had some responsibility for my abuse, my counselor has really thrown me a curve. My first reaction is to feel defensive, and then I feel offended. Even though I had major issues with my dad, ascribing any responsibility to him at all seemed to be a stretch. And suggesting anything mom did was connected to my abuse borders on sacrilege. But as I start looking at certain dynamics from a distance, I see connections. This awareness moves me to attempt the most difficult subject of my therapy: my parents. So close, so personal. So vulnerable, so hurt.

Mom

We gotta talk mom
I'm sure you know by now what the preacher did
I'm also sure you blame yourself
I want you to know
I don't blame you
But some things at home did contribute
You know how you always told me not to be like
      dad?
You overdid it mom
He was my father
I am like him in lots of ways
Telling me to not be like him
Was kinda like telling me to be ashamed of me
I am beginning to find out that I need to accept
The good and bad of him in me

Before I can choose what to keep
And what to throw away

And you know how you always pushed me
To accomplish something every day?
Always be responsible
Gotta see what I achieved
Or else the day was wasted
I finally figured out you can't see love.
Taking the time to just be with
And appreciate others has great value
I worked until I was almost 50
Before I took the time to value those around me
Including my wife and kids
I kept my head down
Working and being responsible like you said
Between that and post-traumatic stress
I missed most of my kids' growing up
And wasn't a lot of help to my wife

You thought the answer was to get me to church
Learn the Christian way
Be around a good influence
Like the preacher
You encouraged me to go as much as possible
Too bad you didn't know what was happening
I was being used
To fulfill a pervert's fantasies
It was bad mom
He twisted all the values you were trying to teach me

Somehow I saved the lessons
You gave me.
I am rebuilding my life based on them
I have a beautiful wife
More beautiful than I ever knew
I have two wonderful daughters

They have grown into impressive women
In spite of me

I have six grandkids
I am trying to do things differently with them
I put my tools down
And stop working when they want my attention
I go to their performances
I think you'd be proud of us all mom
I'm trying to take life less seriously
Even laugh at it… sometimes
We are learning together
Life is getting better
Bummer it took so long to figure it out
Better late than never

I want to mention a couple of special memories
Breakfasts of oatmeal and raisons or rice with cinnamon
And soup and sandwiches for lunch
Just you, grandma and me
Nurture of good food and love

The before-bedtime visits with all of us sitting on your bed
Talking about the day and what it meant
That was the best mom
But no touching
I'm not sure why that was
I could have used some hugs
I wish you had lived longer mom
My life would have been so different
I needed you so badly
But I couldn't admit it to myself
I wasn't grown yet
And I wasn't there for you at the end
I was numb
I never even told you goodbye

Thanks for what you gave me mom
My morals and values came from you
I love you mom
I've missed you a lot

Dealing with the memories of my dad, though, is what causes me to stumble the most. A month or so ago I dreamt that my father was going away forever, maybe dying. I was a little uncomfortable at first because I didn't want to say I loved him when I didn't feel that way. After a few moments, I was able to hug him and say, "take care."

It may not sound like much, but after struggling with my feelings about my father for a lifetime, it is very significant to find an appropriate way to express how I feel about him—no hate and no guilt.

Dad

Okay here we go dad.
Finally looking at our relationship
And what I got from you
I guess relationship is the wrong word
It denotes back and forth
There was no back and forth
Only forth
From your mouth to my ears
Or from the back of your hand
It's too bad there were no computers in your day
I'm sure it would have been easier to program a
        machine
Than it was to train me
I think I got the lessons though
I like the power of positive thinking
It has worked well for me

I've carried "be responsible" a little too far
And the business values never clicked with me

I guess I just don't have your killer instinct
A little concept called fairness seems to stop me

I do like to read
I seem to soak up information the same as you did
Memory is pretty good too
In spite of the drugs

I finally got over "a house is a man's castle" thing
New concept dad
Everybody's equal
Wife and kids have rights too

Of course the big one dad
Observation
Observe and anticipate
I guess all those smacks on the forehead got through
I'm pretty good at it
Although it kind of gets in the way of relationships
People get tired of it
And nobody comes close to our standards dad
I never knew others didn't get the lessons
I just thought it was bad luck
That I kept running into ignorant or inadequate people

I'm having to learn to relax the standards
To allow mere mortals in
It's actually kind of pleasant dad
They have things to offer that you never mentioned

There are a few memories that stick with me dad
I remember getting scared as a little kid
I don't remember your ever helping me feel safe
You never did those male father things either
Fishing once
Camping once
That's it
Lessons and correction daily of course

I remember that time
My sister twice my age teased me
And then ran into the bathroom and locked the door
I lost my temper and kicked a hole in the door
You said it was my fault and I had to pay for it
Only thing was I found out years later
You charged me four times the actual cost
Just to drive the lesson home
To a nine-year-old
I remember real well that night you caught me taking the car
I was 14
I hid in my room
Mom stood at the door
She told you not to use the buckle
I'll never forget your words dad
"Get out of the way Edythe or I'll use it on you"
I don't remember what part of the belt you hit me with
I started screaming before you landed the first blow
It didn't last long and I survived
Reassured of your authority over the family

By the way dad I was an actor in high school
I was in lots of plays
Was even voted best thespian when I graduated
I don't remember you at many of those performances

And the jobs dad
What was up with the jobs?
You always got me jobs
You would tell me where to go
No interview
I'd just show up and start working
Were you like a tough guy?
"Hey my kid needs a job
He'll be here Monday, put him to work"
Was I supposed to say thank you for that?

I remember the first time I brought my future wife to the house
You were sitting in *your* spot in the family room
Beside the table with *your* treats and sweets
Nobody else was allowed to touch
You were in your robe and underwear
I introduced her to you
And you say "want to see my surgery scar?"
You opened your robe with only underwear on
I almost die of embarrassment

After we got married we invited you and mom over for dinner
When you got there you opened the door and walked in
Mom got mad and told you to knock next time
You didn't understand that
Did you dad?

Kind of like when you helped us buy our first house
You saw a couple of things you liked
And took them away before the house deal closed
The whole world was filled with little chess pieces
To be placed wherever you saw fit
Then mom died
What little accountability
You ever had was gone
You started drinking heavily again
And began asking my female friends for dates
Or you would show up at my place of work
Plop your fat ass in the nearest chair
And tell someone to "tell Randy his dad is here"

And why exactly did you feel the need
To tell me you had a mistress?
Not an affair, a mistress
Were you bragging
Or were you modeling for your son
Were you saying that one woman couldn't satisfy you
Or just that mom couldn't

I almost forgot that time we were riding in the car
You were tailgating a fire truck up ahead
The fireman on the back pointed
At the sign that said to not follow close
You rolled your window down and
Pointed to your consular corps license plates
As if that gave you the right
You just saw your place in the world
Different than everyone else did
One of your stunts hurt me more than most
After mom died, her brother gave you money
To cover her funeral and burial
A few years later I went to the cemetery to see mom
I couldn't find her grave
Came to find out you never bought a headstone
Evidently you needed the money for something else
More than you needed to mark the passage of your wife
It took over a decade to come up with money
But I finally got one made

Remember that basketball game I took you to
You told me to park in the handicapped space
Even though I didn't have a sticker
You said you would just tell them you left yours at home

On the way home I tried to talk to you
I told you the family didn't like being around you
When you were drinking
You told me you liked the way you were just fine
If others didn't, that was their problem

There was that memorable Thanksgiving
Helen told you not to bring your fancy turkey-ham
Alternating slices of ham and turkey
You had some poor butcher make for you
She wanted to bake a real turkey
Well you showed up not only with the turkey-ham

But also presents for everyone
And you expected us all to drop what we were doing
And come sit in front of you so you could bestow your gifts

Then during dinner, the coup de grace dad
One of your best
You got a bloody nose and left the table
You came back with wads of bloody toilet paper in both nostrils
As you satiated yourself
You didn't even notice that none of us finished our dinner

I tried to distance myself from you for a few years
Then after prodding and a good dose of guilt
I offered to take you up to our cabin for the night
When I got there to pick you up you had "loaded up" for the trip
You couldn't walk and I had to help you to the car
When we arrived I helped you inside and went to build a fire
You fell down on your back and couldn't get up
You told me to just get a pillow and leave you there
An hour later I helped you up and out to the car, and back home again
You never did see the cabin except from the floor
You would have liked it dad

I don't want to remember all the times we cleaned up your apartment
I usually took a truckload to the dump
With all your papers and rotten food
Your fridges were so bad
They might have sprouted legs and walked out

Then your friends started calling
You needed help
Said you shouldn't be on your own anymore
I was supposed to do something about it
They didn't get it
You had chosen your life

 We ended up moving you to assisted living
That worked for what dad—
A few weeks?

Then they started calling
To say you were being disruptive in the dining hall
Next was the call from the taxi driver you hired
To go buy you a case of half gallons of vodka
A bottle with skim milk every two days dad
And when you couldn't pay
You told him to call me and I would take care of it

Then they called and said you had to leave
You were no longer welcome

I came and had a talk
Remember dad
I said if you didn't go into treatment
I was leaving and you would never hear from me again

So at age 85 you went to the hospital
You lost it while you were there
You were so accustomed to being drunk
Your mind just couldn't handle sober
We put you in a nursing home
And the first thing you did was escape out a window
You ended up in the hospital with gangrene in your leg
I told them not to operate dad

You died a couple of weeks later
With you gone dad
A little balance returned to the earth

I don't know where this all leaves us dad
I'm not sure what our relationship meant to you
But it has caused a mountain of anxiety and shame
To lie knotted inside me all my life

Half of my genetic makeup comes from you
It contributes to my strengths and weaknesses
So does my path that curves to avoid your unpleasantries
Humanity gone amuck
For now I will accept that you are part of me
Someday I may find a way to understand and accept you

Chapter 17

neglected loved ones

As I reflect on my life, it seems now that I have been traveling at a 20-degree list to starboard. It takes a lot of concentration to be that off-kilter and appear normal. It certainly limited my ability to deal effectively with the challenges of relationships, parenting and career. To make people think there is nothing wrong with you, you have to try to maintain close to the same degree of list at all times. Believe me it's not easy. I feel remorse about my lack of attention to my family and others who depended on me when I was too busy maintaining my lie. Now I have spent over two years in therapy dealing with me, talking about me, feeling sorry for me, focused on me. You have to do that to recover from something like this. You won't ever get well if you don't.

But now it's time to broaden my scope. My life, with all of its distortions, affected many others. How does a 57-year-old man go forward after discovering his life has been based on denial that drove him to extremes even he did not know existed? What comes to mind are the eighth and ninth steps of Alcoholics Anonymous: "make a list of all people we have harmed, and become willing to make amends to them; make direct amends to such people wherever possible, except when to do so would injure them or others." Right now I can only attempt this with my immediate family. Anything more just seems too overwhelming.

A man immersed in his victimhood thinks only of himself and his pain. Even after years of therapy, I have been slow to realize how my distortions affected those around me, the ones I am closest to. Finally I am beginning to recognize this, admit it to them, and attempt to make amends.

These next few pages contain my apologies, if you will, to my family. I have been advised by my editors to leave them out of the book. As has often been the case in my life, I am not going to heed their advice. I can't. If I leave this part out, you will not realize how important my family is to me, or that they are a primary reason for my recovering at all. If not for them, I could just go off somewhere and stay stoned for the rest of my life. I also hope this reminds other survivors that we do not live in a vacuum. Our "surviving" takes a toll on those around us. Loving is give and take. I have done more than my share of taking. Now it's time to start giving.

Maggie May

My beautiful baby girl
It was so hot that day you were born
You didn't want to come out
So the doctor broke moms water
He went back to his office
You came so fast then
He almost didn't make it back
To deliver you

You were such a quiet baby
No bother at all
I don't think you wanted to inconvenience
        anybody
I can't believe we smoked in the room you slept in
Probably why you still get that cough
I remember when you learned to walk
We were at the coast in a rental house
You needed your Mickey Mouse ears
And your little red purse to stay on your feet
Missing either one
Down you went

When Mom went to Portland
To finish college
You just couldn't handle the change
So you came home and stayed with me
While your sister stayed with your mom

You and I took that trip to Baker
To see Uncle Steve
We drove the Audi Fox
And listened to Linda Ronstadt
"Love is a Rose"
The whole way there and back

I remember in kindergarten
Mrs. Littman had to tell the whole class
To be quiet so they could hear
What Maggie had to say
Because you were so soft spoken
And of course you never wanted to
Do anything to get into twuble

Your first day of first grade
You were so cute in your little dress
Seems like it was turquoise
You were so excited and scared
All at the same time

One of my proudest moments
As a parent
Was your seventh grade conference
When we sat down the teacher said
Oh, Maggie's parents
I thought uh oh
Here we go
She went on to tell us how
You had been part of the "in crowd"
But you had stepped away
When they made fun of other kids
She said you took a stand
To support Larry who had special needs
And others who were not considered "cool"

She told us how rare that was
And what an exceptional person you were

She was right you know, you are rare
I was so impressed and proud
We didn't connect a lot after that
One part because you were a teenager
Four parts because I just wasn't available
And when I was
You were usually pissed at me for not being there
When you needed me
So now we find ourselves at odds a lot

I can't even begin to know
All the times and ways I let you down
I hope you get over being mad at me
And will be able to forgive me some day
I really want to be close to you
And for you to be able to trust me
You have grown up
So beautiful, talented and strong
But to me you will always be
My beautiful baby girl

And now for my oldest daughter, who took a lot of the brunt of my dysfunction.

Cachita

You were the most agreeable baby ever
You had a smile for everyone
The only time you ever got mad
Was when you had to go to bed
You never wanted to miss anything
You didn't even mind
When you had casts on your feet to straighten them
And you were the most verbal baby anybody ever saw
Complete sentences before you were two

Adolescence took a toll on us
We fought a lot

I was so authoritarian
And you fought back with everything you had
Which was considerable
Funny though
You have always gone your own way
When you became a mom
You were the best mom you knew how to be

We still fought
And you always stood up to me
No bend
No compromise
Wonder where you learned that
It took me a long time to come to respect you
But I finally did

When I told you about my past
You cried and hugged me
Then you looked at me and said
"It all makes sense now dad, everything"
My seer
The one who sees
What others don't even know is there

I watch others judge you harshly
You don't always do what they think proper
And of course you carry their judgment
And let it taint how you feel about yourself
Just like I taught you

They just think
Everyone should be in a box like theirs
They don't know what it's like
To see and hear and know what you do
It's like juggling seven or eight balls
Instead of one or two like the rest of us
The pressure and focus it takes to hold it
     together

Would crush lesser people
I'd like to teach you a new way
Leave what belongs to others with them
It is enough to be true to yourself
Don't you worry

Thank you for your understanding
And for your help in my healing
I know I have a lot of making up to do
Maybe over time
Your resentment will soften
I will keep trying
And I will keep learning to do better
I promise

Blessings to you
And your gifts

And now for the most difficult, most painful shame I need to own. I ask
for the forgiveness of my partner and wife who has been with me since we
were eighteen years old. In running from the truth and protecting myself, I
contributed to her own sense of powerlessness, the same powerlessness I felt as
a victim. I didn't know any other way. I was flying blind, trying to be an adult,
but stuck at age 15 in so many ways.

Helen

Where do I start
Do I apologize for the lies about me
And who I really was
Or should I start with a heartfelt apology
For the lackluster attitude
I brought into our marriage
I think both are important now

The most self-centered thing of all
When I needed to flee Portland
I never gave a thought

To the impact on your life
Just one more year of college
Your dream of becoming a teacher
Gone in a flash

Grab your coat
And your one-year-old baby
Follow your victim husband
Into the mountains
Your aspirations and dreams
Dust
My God how could I have been so selfish

That move changed the course of your life
More than mine
For me it was just one of many careers
You became a cook
Instead of a teacher
You were stuck
For over twenty years
How do I make up for something like that?

Our next stop
Was Bend
I worked long hours
Including weekends
Began drinking heavily

Left you and the kids
To fend for yourselves
Then we went broke
And lost our home

After plenty of suffering
A new plan emerged
Yank the kids out of school
And away from their friends
Move back to Portland

And let everybody start over
(Especially me)
I think that one almost destroyed the kids
I was happy to be back
I assumed you liked it too
But never asked until now
And you told me you never wanted to leave Bend
I'm pretty sure I didn't notice
What it did to the girls
And if I did I just figured they needed to buck up
That's life you know
We have to sacrifice
For the good of the family
Or in this case, as always
For the sake of dad
I don't think they ever recovered
But you and I did
Especially after things got good at work
We started traveling
And having some fun together

That came to an end as well
I got dissatisfied
And needed to move on again
You didn't want to leave your life and friends
But again I insisted
So you followed me to Southern Oregon
Where you have lived
In another half-dozen houses

And just to make it real special
You got to live through
My gutting them and remodeling them
Usually with only one room
Safe from my wrecking ball
Thoughtful of me
Don't you think?

When those houses were done and pretty
We sold them and started over
You must love me a lot
To have given up so much
Just to stay with me
I'm pretty sure I didn't deserve it
People are impressed that we have been married
For 38 years
I have taken pride in that
I realize now
I had nothing to do with it
It was you
All you

And now after everything else
You have stayed with me
Through four years of recovery
Aren't you sick of it yet?
I feel like a changed person
But I am just beginning to "get it"
I have never really understood
And still you are with me
I cannot begin to fathom how lucky I am
In all seriousness I don't deserve you

It seems impossible to imagine
After all this
That I might
Actually get smarter
But I promise
I am going to try

I am shocked by an epiphany
As I put these words on paper
There is nothing in my life
More important than you

I am going to try start acting like it
I know I can never make it all up to you
But maybe
Just maybe
I can begin to show you
How special you really are to me
My Love
My Life

Chapter 18

mediation

In February 2008 I am told mediation will happen in early May. Then, in March, I am told the court date has been pushed out to the end of the month at the latest. By April, the date has slipped again to the first of July at the latest. One major stumbling block is that The Church's insurance carriers claim they have no liability and therefore won't take part. The Church can't or won't mediate without the back up insurance. In July, the court orders the insurance people to at least attend the mediation hearing and to find a date that will work for everyone. At last, mediation is set for the end of October. The waiting feels like hanging out to dry.

I try to use the time to prepare myself. Deal with my *stuff*. Put the victim in me away. I think I am ready for it all. I tell the counselor I am confident in who I am and have faith in God to bring a fair and just resolution.

Mediation Week

Mediation is four days away
I drank for the last three nights
One night, a pint of whiskey
First time in months.
Over this same period
I have been eating like a gluttonous pig
After being on a diet for four weeks
Last week at counseling
I told my counselor I was ready
I could handle it
Ha! Fool!

Two and half years ago I started therapy
Two years ago I filed a formal complaint with the church
A year and half ago I filed a lawsuit
Over that entire period I have worked on healing
My body and my spirit
Now with one week to go
Seven lousy days
I come unhinged
Abandoning all that I have learned
About myself and life
Rushing back to being a victim
And finding solace in numbing my emotions
As I've done for 40 years
I don't get it
What am I afraid of?

What is it in the process
That scares me?
The room full of lawyers?
The Mediators?
The Bishop?
That I will not be understood?
That I will be made a victim again?
That justice will not be served?
Or that this struggle will be over
Regardless of how it turns out
I really don't know

So now I ask myself
What do I want out of this?
First I have to admit
I want restitution
I want somebody to pay me back for the life I lost
I want the church to quit keeping secrets
I want them to tell what happened
Look for other victims

And make amends as best they can
I want them to openly advocate for child victims

I want them to start the dialog
That will help people report abuse
Seek professional help after being abused
Teach kids how to avoid being victims

There's more
I want the church to take a leadership role
In talking about the problem
Get it out in the open
Help pass laws to protect children
And put perpetrators and pedophiles
Behind bars
It's going to take us all
To stop this un-Godly epidemic

Am I scared that none of this will happen?
Am I scared that only part of it will happen?
I don't really have time to be scared
The time for fear is over
My time for being a victim is over
It's time for passion and getting to work
To see that change happens

Two Days to Go

Two days before mediation
My therapist daughter
Comes over to give Helen and me massages
Helen goes first
When my turn comes
I tell her I want to read a poem I wrote
About my grandma before she starts
I play grandma's favorite hymn
"How Great Thou Art"
While I read

As I finish, my psychic daughter becomes startled and says,
 "Um, dad, the room is filled with dead people
Probably 30 of them
In a circle around you.
Ancestors three generations back
Have come to give their support
Some have regrets about their choices in life
But they are all here to help you seek justice
And to protect you as they did not
When you were young and vulnerable."

I never did get the massage
But I did get the message
We talked and visited
As she told me what they were passing on to her
Not in words but feelings
What she said fit their personalities
And had the ring of truth
Even though most were dead long before she was born
The most powerful emotion
From just a couple of them was
The feeling of regret
I'm thinkin' there's a message there

Now I don't care whether you believe in spirits or not
I think I do
I can't begin to tell you
What strength and peace it gave me
Knowing that my ancestors
Were going into that mediation with me

May I always remember
They are there with me
Whenever I need them

My lawyer tells me to be available for two days of mediation, so we drive
300 miles and stay in a motel the day before. My wife drives while I listen to

my music and attempt to meditate and center myself. I do pretty well, but "attempt" is the key word. I go to bed early and get up at seven in order to meet my attorney at eight for breakfast, as if I could actually put any food in my stomach.

Ground Zero

So the time has finally come
After what feels like years
Or at least a lifetime
I go to the courthouse
With my attorney
He told me to bring a book
Now I know why
We are sitting in a huge empty courtroom
After about an hour
A casually dressed 60-year-old man comes in
Sits down and starts talking about football and golf
He is a retired judge, and the mediator

My attorney has prepared me
Don't be offended, this is how they do it
A half hour later the mediator gets up and says
Gotta go mix it up with the suits
And leaves the room

He and his partner
Another mediator and judge
Come in just before noon
Sit down to "visit"
Then tell us to go to lunch
And be back in an hour

Arriving back from lunch
We stand in the lobby
And count 12 suits
An even dozen
Attorneys for the church

And the three insurance companies
That's a lot of coverage
I'll bet if you stripped them all down to their skivvies
Sold all the suits
You could feed and house
All the homeless in my town for a year

The mediators come in and "visit" a couple of times
I hardly see my ancestor's spirits
I figure they're off in the rooms with the lawyers
Working inside their heads

Around 4:30
They come in and apologize
Say go home and come back tomorrow at nine
I am tired and drained
This process has been going on for over 18 months
I just want it to be over

The next day in the courthouse lobby
We wait for the doors to be unlocked
Somebody has sent an extra "suit"
Now there is a bakers' dozen (13)

Yesterday I was able to read
Today I cannot focus
We hardly see the mediators
At noon they stop in to say it's not going well
The insurance companies are denying coverage
They may not be able to get an offer together
But it *is* Friday afternoon
So don't leave the building
Get a snack downstairs

Around four o'clock the mediators come in
And plop exhausted into chairs
They have an offer
Not great but respectable
One of the mediators looks and me

With the greatest sincerity says
Nobody deserves to have happen to them
What happened to you
And no amount of money can make up for it

I had decided months ago that it would end here
Whatever was offered I would take
It isn't just about money
It is about justice and taking a stand
I agree to take the money offered
As long as I can meet with the bishop

The Bishop and I are taken to a room alone
I had prepared my requests
He apologizes to me
I'm not sure
If it's for what happened to me as a boy
Or for how this whole process has gone
I take it for both

He comes off gentle and kind
We have a meeting of the minds
He promises to do everything in his power
To fulfill my requests
We talk for an hour
He commits to a meeting with me within two weeks
Then we pray

The mediators say if it doesn't work out
They will set a new date and mediate my requests
We are done

I walk out of the courthouse in a daze
Back to my hotel and to my wife
I am so weepy it is hard to talk
Validation?
Completion?
Emotional release?
Letdown?

A week later he writes to say the first request is done. Full disclosure has been made in all the churches where Reverend Ron served and letters will be sent to all parishioners as well. After our first talk he even changed his vernacular from "an incident of sexual misconduct" to sexual abuse of a child. Score one small victory for victims. We set a date and time to meet again. Two weeks later I travel to Portland for my follow-up meeting with the Bishop.

A Good Start

I was all pumped up
For my next meeting with the Bishop
We would talk about correction and prevention
Turn around my abuse
Have it mean something
Do some good

I spend the two weeks looking for teaching aids
For Sunday school teachers
Curriculum they call it
Not much out there
But I find some
Pay an extra 30 bucks to ship by air
Just to get it in time.
The stuff was better than I thought
Damn good
I go to the meeting pretty excited
Gonna change the world don't ya know
He glances at the material
Thinks it is a bit much
Says it might work for a camp setting
Which is to say
Not for Sunday school

I put my sellin' shoes on
Try to tell him how surprised I was when I read it all
Bein' a victim doesn't start by accident
We learn it

So we gotta teach kids how not to be victims
Teach things like self-respect
And mutual respect
Learn to have healthy relationships
Teach that we have the right to protect our private space
And so does everybody else
Teach folks to stand up to bullies
Not just be a bystander

He got it
But he doesn't buy it
Bums me out

It is a good meeting though
He will do what he can
To implement the programs we discussed
I think we connect on two out of three issues
Guess I expected it all
Don't happen that way
There's some sayin'
'Bout buildin' Rome in a day

In June 2009, six months after my meetings with the Bishop, I received an email detailing the following legislation that had just passed as church law at the state conference. These standards will now be implemented in 210 churches with over thirty thousand members in two states.

Minimum Standards for Abuse Awareness

Abuse comes in many forms and occurs in many ways and in many places. Prevention of emotional, physical, verbal and sexual abuse is vitally important to us as Christians. Children, youth and adults hear about abuse and abuse prevention in school and in public media. It is important for all to know that their church is vitally concerned with their well-being as children of God. Abuse Prevention Month is observed nationally in April and could be an appropriate time for a faith focus on abuse as well.

continued on next page...

...continued from previous page

The following are MINIMUM standards for raising awareness about abuse. Each local church ministry setting shall:

1. annually designate one Sunday on which abuse awareness and abuse prevention are incorporated into the worship experience.

2. annually offer an educational opportunity for children, youth, and/or adults on abuse prevention.

3. make available resource materials on abuse prevention for children, youth and adults for use in local ministry settings.

4. request clergy to report annually to the all-church conference ways in which minimum standards for abuse awareness were met.

Supporting Information

Why is it important?

1. We have learned through media coverage, lawsuits, growing national concern, and the experience of survivors of abuse in our congregations that abuse is not only sexual but also emotional and verbal; that men are not the only abusers but also women, children, and youth; that victims are not only women and children, but men as well.

2. An intentional focus on abuse awareness and prevention allows congregations to be in ministry with abuse survivors: encouraging them to seek help or counseling as well as providing an outlet for them to help others identify and avoid abusive situations.

3. Churches are the ideal place for children, youth, and adults to develop healthy relationships and strong families through faith-based programs that emphasize good communication, respect for others, healthy personal boundaries, peaceful problem solving, and good use of personal resources. Churches can reinforce personal strength as a base for children, youth, and adults to

continued on next page...

...continued from previous page

be aware of the potential for abuse in such forms as domestic violence, bullying, peer pressure, sexual violence, and internet abuse.

4. Our Church Social Principles "affirm that sexuality is God's good gift to all persons" and that all are called "to responsible stewardship of this sacred gift." We believe "that all persons are individuals of sacred worth, created in the image of God" and that "the Church should support the family in providing age-appropriate education regarding sexuality to children, youth, and adults."

Blessings on those individuals who worked on this beautiful and comprehensive document. It is not only well said, but it demands accountability, which is the only way to change the system.

New policies and laws are being enacted around the country because victims have come forward to tell their stories. As difficult as this whole process has been, I would not eliminate any of it. I could not. The journey is changing my entire existence and the lives of countless others. Telling our truth not only changes our own lives, it impacts the world in ways we cannot possibly anticipate.

Epilogue

moving forward

After my realization of how much my dysfunction had ruled my being, I know that to give my life meaning, I have to do something to help others heal. The life skills I have learned in my many careers, and in overcoming my victimization, have prepared me to make a difference. I have decided to become a victims' advocate. After the struggle of the last three years on the road to recovery, I believe I can be fearless in responding to any opportunity that comes along.

A year ago I saw an article in the paper about a woman who was walking from one end of the state to the other to bring awareness to sexual abuse. Her daughter had been abused as a child, but Oregon's statute of limitations had run out. The woman was angry and wanted to do something, anything, to help her daughter. She was afraid of retributions against her daughter, so she was using a pseudonym and wearing a wig and sunglasses.

I got up that morning and drove to the Albertson's parking lot where the walk was to start. I approached the woman (whom I'll call "Meredith") and introduced myself. I told her I wanted to walk with her. After Meredith got over her shock at my showing up, she gave me a bright yellow T-shirt that proclaimed "Stop Child Sex Abuse" in bold black lettering. One other woman was with her, and the three of us started walking, sharing our stories along the way. People stopped us on the street to encourage us, and some proceeded to share their stories.

Although I didn't quite make it the full ten miles that day, I did join Meredith on two more days of her 30-day hike. I was both gratified and surprised when cars and trucks honked encouragement as we walked along the highway. The overt support from the construction and logging trucks was an even greater shock. It didn't seem like much of a commitment on my part, but it felt good to step out for the first time.

Meredith later got a state representative to sponsor a bill before the Oregon State Legislature to extend the statute of limitations for civil action against child sexual abusers. Advocating for that extension, I testified before the Senate Judiciary Committee along with two other victim/survivors. Later that day, I found myself being televised on the six o'clock news in the city where I had lived most of my life. Over the next few weeks, I heard from people I hadn't talked to in years. Some were shocked. Some just said "way to go."

A few religious groups organized in opposition to the bill. Apparently they felt the bill might increase their liability. On the day of the vote, one Senator got up and gave an impassioned and courageous speech about the abuse she suffered as a child. She ended it by recounting how her cousin, who had also been abused, had committed suicide after years of prostitution. After a close vote, the bill passed and became law in January 2010.

A few months later I attended a rally to bring awareness to child abuse. The local director of United Way had been on jury duty earlier in the year, an experience that brought a stream of abuse cases to her attention. She was shocked into action and organized this rally as a starting point. Ten local professionals—school principals, judges, and social workers—stood up one at a time and read children's own stories of their trauma. Following the rally, I walked up to the United Way director and slipped a poem I had written into her hand. The poem was about stopping abuse. I turned and walked away, too embarrassed and scared to speak.

A couple of months later, I went to see the director, who said she had been trying to find out who I was. We visited and she told me about a group she was starting called CAN, Child Abuse Network. We have since become friends and I am now a member of CAN and attend meetings monthly. Working with the local newspaper and a TV station, CAN initiated a public awareness event called "Don't Turn Away."

Out of my work with CAN came an opportunity to become a trained facilitator for Darkness To Light (www.darkness2light.org). The program, directed at parents, teachers, and church groups, is designed to increase awareness of child sexual abuse, how to help prevent it, and how to facilitate recovery.

I am also working as a member of OAASIS, Oregon Abuse Advocates and Survivors in Service (www.oaasisoregon.org), an organization that emerged from the group that had worked to pass the extension to Oregon's statute of limitations. OAASIS is a nonprofit coalition of individuals and organizations formed to increase public awareness. We have developed a Survivors Speakers Bureau of male and female survivors and family members to go out and share the real-life impact of child sex abuse. OAASIS has established a Political Action Committee that interviews candidates for state office and works for those who support our agenda. Members of OAASIS also lobby to change laws to make it easier for victims to come forward and find justice and put perpetrators behind bars. We are currently working on new legislation to impact the issue of Human Sex Trafficking. A new opportunity has miraculously dropped from heaven. A legislator has introduced a bill to eliminate the criminal statute of limitations for sexual abuse of children in Oregon. Something that was only a distant dream may become reality, if we can get our lawmakers to understand the scope of this heinous crime.

I also want to make a difference with my own family—my wife Helen, and my children and grandchildren. When I was not at work, I probably gave them 20 percent of my time over the years. I intend to make up for that now, by being with them more and being a much different person when we are together: living straight and sober, learning patient attentiveness, offering love and support. What a difference that is. What a difference it will be.

Shed the Shame

Since I started speaking out
Lot's o' people
Been comin' up
And talkin' all secret like
Some even whisper
Tellin' me what happened in their family
To them, their husbands, papas or sons

It occurs to me
It ain't okay in so-ciety
To tell these things to nobody
We think people don't want to hear
And then there's the biggie
SHAME

If you or your child had a horrible disease
Or were hurt in an accident
You would have no fear of sharing
Neighbors would bring over a casserole
Empathy would flow freely

But nay
With sexual abuse of our children
We go inside
Close the windows and blinds
Keep the secret
The shame of the abuser
Is worn by the victim

Perhaps it is time for release
Open the windows and doors
Tell the secret
Set the victim
And the family free
Validate what happened to him or her
Tell them it is not
Nor was it ever
Their fault
We understand
And honor them
And their loss

the music

Throughout my healing process, I listened to music. Music brought on sadness and melancholy with memories, but it also lifted my spirits when I was low and gave me strength to go on when I didn't think I could. Although I owe a huge debt of gratitude to all the artists who created this music, three musicians were key to my recovery. Maria Muldaur, Eric Bibb, and Ruthie Foster, whether you know it or not, your music helps heal the soul. It has been as important to my recovery as my counseling sessions. Because of music's significance, I want to share what I have come to call my "Good Stuff" songs. I have put these songs onto CDs that I have listened to over and over (much to my wife's chagrin).

This music works for me. It may or may not do anything for you. These songs appeal to my 1960s idealism and my simple faith. You may find other music that appeals and uplifts you. Use it freely and often to help your recovery, or when you find you are feeling lower than a rug and not really a member of the human race.

Brothers and Sisters

Eric Bibb, Maria Muldaur, Rory Black

"Don't Ever Let Nobody Drag Your Spirit Down"
"Give A Little More"
"My Sisters and Brothers"
"Get Up, Get Ready"

Yes We Can

Maria Muldaur, Jenni Muldaur, The Free Radicals, Women's Voices for Peace Choir, Holly Near, Joel Jaffe, Suzy Thompson, Linda Tillery, Bonnie Raitt, Eric Thompson, Jane Fonda, Anne Lamott, Marianne Williamson, Jean Shinda Bolen, Kimberly Bass

"Make a Better World"
"Yes We Can"
"This Old World"
"We Shall Be Free"
"Down by the Riverside"

Runaway Soul — Ruthie Foster
"Woke Up This Mornin' "
"Hole in My Pocket"
"Walk On"
"Joy"

"Redemption Song" Bob Marley

"Share the Land" The Guess Who

"With My Own Two Hands" Ben Harper, Jack Johnson

"Peace Train" Yusuf Islam (Cat Stevens)

"Hallelujah" k.d. lang

"Lord of the Dance" Donovan

"Down to the River to Pray" Alison Krauss *Oh Brother Where Art Thou?*

"Simple Things" Judy Collins

"Morning Has Broken" Cat Stevens

"We Shall Overcome" Bruce Springsteen *Where Have All the Flowers Gone*

"How Beautiful Upon the Mountain" Tom Paxton *Comedians and Angels*

"Peace Will Come" Tom Paxton *Your Shoes My Shoes*

"Heather's Song" Misty River *Live at the Backgate Stage*

"Imagine" John Lennon

"Everybody Be Yoself" Keb Mo *Big Wide Grin*

"The Cape" Eric Bibb, Martin Simpson *Eric Bibb and Friends*

"Needed Time" Eric Bibb, Harry Manx *Eric Bibb and Friends*

"If I Had My Way" Peter, Paul and Mary

"Wedding Song" Peter, Paul and Mary

"Somewhere Over the Rainbow/What a Wonderful World" Brudda Iz

"What More Can I Say" Nina Simone

"You Are So Beautiful" Joe Cocker

"Americassong"   Will.I.Am, Faith Hill, Seal, Mary J Bilge, Bono

"Stand By Me" Playing for Change-Song Around the World

"How Great Thou Art" Chris Rice

about the author

Randy Ellison is a victim's advocate and activist for cultural change regarding child sexual abuse. He speaks publicly to all types of groups, at fundraisers and at rallies. He also testifies before state legislatures and lobbies these bodies regarding changes to our legal system for the benefit of victims and survivors.

Randy works with several organizations on abuse prevention and awareness. He is a member of CAN, Child Abuse Network in Medford, Oregon, which is a collaboration of over 40 agencies working together to impact child abuse in Southern Oregon. He is also Board President of OAASIS, Oregon Abuse Advocates and Survivors in Service, based in Portland, Oregon. OAASIS is a non-profit whose mission is to protect children from sexual abuse and to empower survivors through public awareness, education and advocacy.

Randy helped change the civil statue of limitations on sex abuse of children to one of the most liberal in the country. He is currently advocating with others to help pass the first Human Sex Trafficking laws in Oregon. Also in the works is a bill to eliminate of the criminal statute of limitations on sexual abuse of children.

Randy lives in Southern Oregon with his wife Helen. He likes to rebuild old houses, go camping and spend time with his grandkids (not necessarily in that order!).

**Visit Randy's website at http://www.boysdonttell.com/.
You can contact him at randy@boysdonttell.com .**

Printed in the USA
CPSIA information can be obtained
at www.ICGtesting.com
JSHW082212140824
68134JS00014B/581

9 781614 480464